THE FI METRIC

Financial Independence. Measure It. Improve It!

fimetric

ERIC G. HOLLAND, CPA, EA

DEDICATION

For my sister Terrilyn. Thank you for inspiring me.
Your courage and grace will forever live in my heart.

CONTENTS

INTRODUCTION

"In the beginner's mind there are many possibilities. In the expert's mind there are few."

~Shunryu Suzuki

If you're tired of the usual drivel that you've been reading in other personal finance books then you've come to the right place. This book will introduce you to a totally new way of looking at your finances. Just about every other book on personal finance boils down to the same old routine. Create an emergency fund, cut your expenses, pay off your debt, save 15% of your income and wait 40 years to see where you end up. They take two or three hundred pages to say it, but that pretty much summarizes their plan for success. Same old same old. This is the best that our financial experts currently have to offer.

Our financial experts are like our politicians. When political campaign season rolls around we voters always try to make it clear that we are tired of the career politicians. They've been in office too long and they just can't relate to the everyday person any longer. They've become ineffective at their jobs. I think the same thing has happened with our financial experts. They've been in office too long and they seem to be more interested in selling books than they are in finding new ideas for us to work with. They make their living by selling books and DVD's, not by earning a paycheck like the rest of us. They have become ineffective at their jobs. It's all grown very stale. Our financial experts are stuck in a rut. Establish your emergency fund, pay off your debt, invest 15% of your income in a Roth IRA. Those may be good ideas, but we've heard it all before. For gosh sakes, we've heard it a thousand times. Can't they come up with something new?

It's time for some new blood. It's time for a fresh new perspective. And that is exactly what you will get with this book. I'm not a life-long financial expert. I'm a regular person with a regular job. By profession,

I'm a software developer. I've spent 20 years building a career as a developer and manager. It's been a great career. But about 6 years ago I got interested in personal finance. I went all in and got the best training and credentials that I could. I think my background gives me a unique slant on things. A way of seeing things differently than the current lot of financial experts. That perspective has led me to develop a financial system that works for me. It's been refined to the point where it's now time to share it with others. This book is all about that system.

What you will find in this book is a fresh new way of managing, monitoring and improving your finances. What you will not find is advice on how to invest in stocks or how to start a business or advance your career. That is not what I'm writing about. The system in this book is a framework for you to go out and build your own financial success. The framework gives you a solid structure within which to operate. You will have to work within the framework to develop your own detailed plan for success. You are in charge. We are all different and we all need to find our own paths to follow.

Think of this system as your vehicle along the path to financial success. It is the best vehicle that you will find. It's solid, fast and reliable. It's the Bugatti Veyron of financial frameworks. If you're not familiar with the Bugatti, it is the fastest street car in the world. It's an amazing car with a top speed of 268 miles per hour. But it doesn't drive itself. It needs a competent driver behind the wheel. Likewise, you need to take the wheel of your financial future. This new system will provide the ultimate framework for financial success. You need to take control of applying that framework. Your skill and determination combined with a solid financial framework is the perfect formula to maximize your chances of success. So strap yourself in and grab the wheel. It's time to learn about the revolutionary new metric that could change your financial future. Happy driving!

CHAPTER 1
THE FI METRIC FRAMEWORK

"Everything should be made as simple as possible, but not simpler. "

~Albert Einstein

It's been said that you can't manage what you can't measure. Since financial independence is an important goal in personal finances, you would think that by now someone would have a way to measure it. Just take a stroll through your local bookstore or do a search on Amazon.com and you will see hundreds of books about financial independence and financial freedom. What you will not find is anyone who can tell you how to *measure* your financial independence. Shelf after shelf full of books by renowned authors–Orman, Trump, Ramsey, Bach, Kiyosaki, Chatzky. Surely one of them must know how to measure the thing that they claim to be experts at. Amazingly, no. Those authors can go on and on about their opinion on what you should do to get your financial independence. But the sad truth is that not a single one of them can give you the tools to measure, monitor and improve your financial freedom. They can tell you about their rich dads and poor dads, how to stand in your truth, how to put things on automatic pilot, or how to get your debt snowball rolling. But they cannot tell you how to monitor and track your financial independence.

And if they can't measure it, then how well do you think they really understand it? Can they define what it is? Can they tell you what creates independence? Can they give you a metric to accurately measure it and a plan to monitor it? No, I'm afraid not. They can't tell you how to measure and monitor the very subject that they have been working with for years or even decades.

And, you'll have no better luck from the well trained and highly respected academics either. The folks who specialize in theories and formulas have come up empty on this one. I have a degree in finance. I have a certificate in financial planning. I've passed the CFP® exams. I'm an enrolled agent and a CPA. I've had a *lot* of training. And I have the grey hairs to prove it. But throughout all of that training, not a single textbook, not a single instructor, not any source whatsoever has ever come close to showing me how to measure financial independence. They talk about it a lot, but they don't define it and they don't offer a metric to monitor it.

I have a textbook in my library from one of the courses that I took. It's titled *Personal Financial Planning: Theory and Practice.* The darn thing is almost 900 pages packed full of juicy information on personal finances and financial planning. I flip open the front section of the book and it has twenty names listed as contributors. They have all kinds of credentials after their names: EA, CFP®, MBA, PHD, PFS, JD, LLM. You name it, they got it. Surely somewhere in those nearly 900 pages, one of these geniuses must have a definition of financial independence, right? They must have a formula to measure it tucked away on one of those pages, don't they? Nope!

I flip to the end of the book and I see a 28-page alphabetical glossary with definitions for all kinds of terms. It starts with *adhesion,* then skips forward to *boot* and *dividend* … all the way to the end where it lists *yield to maturity.* But right in between *financial goals,* and *financial mission,* right where they should have a definition for financial independence, what do they have? White space. Seriously, here is the proof:

Financial Accounting Standards Board (FASB) - nongovernmental board that sets standards for financial statements and generally accepted accounting principles (GAAP).

financial goals - high level statements of financial desire that may be for the short run or the long run.

financial mission - a broad and enduring statement that identifies the client's long-term purpose for wanting a financial plan.

What should have been the most important definition in the whole book is glaringly absent. Call me crazy, but I think a book titled *Personal Financial Planning: Theory and Practice* ought to have a definition for financial independence. But no, it's not there. I can't find that definition in *any* of my personal finance books. So, why is it missing? I think it's missing because these people just don't understand it. They are thinking too academically and not pragmatically enough. How can you mentor people on a subject that you don't know how to measure or monitor? How can you advise people on a subject if you can't define it?

What a sad miserable state for the financial planning industry to be in. After all of my training, after all of my study, after all of my research, I have come to a conclusion. Traditional financial planning is broken. I've wasted a lot of time and money studying the works of a bunch of really smart people who have just flat-out missed the target. Don't get me wrong, there are some brilliant people out there. I've learned some powerful formulas and techniques for financial planning. But the most important formula from a personal finance perspective is missing. Without a formula for financial independence, how can you plan for it?

Traditional financial planning is broken.

A lot of those financial books stress the importance of setting measurable goals. And then they go on to talk about the importance of financial independence. Well, clearly, something is missing. If financial independence is an important goal, and setting measurable goals is important to success, then I think we need a way to measure financial independence. When I started my journey studying personal finance, I thought that I would find all of the important answers along the way. I didn't expect to find a big empty doughnut hole in the middle of everything. But that is what I found. Air, gas, empty space. The great abyss of financial planning.

Let me save you from wasting your valuable time on those kinds of studies. Let me save you from spending your money on books and materials that won't address the root of the financial planning problem. Forget traditional financial planning. It's broken. Forget retirement planning. It's too passive. Instead, let's do some "freedom planning". Let's put a plan into action that actually effectuates change. A plan that will increase your financial independence month after month. Let's get a plan with a specific, measurable goal of becoming financially independent. A plan that includes continuous measuring and monitoring. A plan that is dynamic so that it can change as needed. Those old methods are now outdated. I wouldn't dream of using that old school stuff. I don't use it myself, and I won't recommend it to anyone else. There is a better way.

I've created a new system for managing personal finances. This new system is a financial framework created out of my own necessity. I needed it for two reasons. First, I needed it for myself. I wanted a way to succeed financially and I did not feel that the current financial planning industry had the answer. I just wasn't satisfied entrusting my financial future to the planning techniques that were available. I didn't want a 40-year plan. I wanted a serious "get it done now" plan. Second, I wanted a system that I believed in enough that I could share it with my clients. I wasn't comfortable talking with people about financial planning using the old methods because I did not believe in them. So, I threw out a lot of the worthless garbage that I learned in school and developed my own system. I took the best of what I learned from my training and combined it with some common sense and some insightful logic. I wasn't interested in being rich. I wasn't interested in having more stuff. What I wanted was to get back into control of my time. I wanted to be financially independent. I wanted freedom.

The framework centers around a metric that can monitor financial independence. I call the metric the FI metric. You pronounce the letters just as they are. As in *eff, eye*. FI stands for Financial Independence. So the FI metric is the Financial Independence metric. I think this metric is so important to financial planning that I created a company called FImetric Corporation.

FImetric Corporation is my business which I use to bring the FI metric to the world. At FImetric, we keep trying to find better ways to put the metric to work for people like you. We provide a great online system which you can use to monitor your finances. It uses state of the art web technologies to provide amazing performance and interactivity. You can find this online system at *http://www.fimetric.com*. Best of all, the system is totally free. The FI metric is incorporated throughout the system. Rather than just balancing your checkbook and tracking your expenses, this system will actually provide valuable feedback and help to keep you on track to becoming financially independent. Go ahead and finish reading this book. It will explain the metric in great detail. Then, after you understand the philosophy behind the system, go online and sign up for your free account.

Most people think financial planning is boring, depressing and frustrating. But I like to keep it fun. I'll be sharing the FI metric system with you throughout this book and I will do my best to throw in a little humor along the way. However, I'm a computer programmer and a CPA so give me a few mercy laughs. As a programmer/CPA, my personality is a cross between Bill Gates and Ben Stein. I'm swimming upstream here so I need all the help I can get.

To help understand how and why the FI metric works, consider other metrics that are frequently used. If you are an investor, then you are no doubt familiar with the PE or price to earnings ratio. PE is a metric that is commonly used for evaluating stocks. FI is kind of like that. It's basically a ratio used to measure a person's financial independence. I'll be explaining the metric to you one step at a time and I'll give you the actual formula to compute it. Not only will I give you a formula to calculate your FI, I will also give you a formula to calculate your FI date. That is the date when your FI will reach 100%. The date when you will become financially free. How cool is that? To think that you can do a projection on your current finances and determine the date when you will become financially independent is a totally new concept. There is no voodoo involved. It's all mathematics.

This is groundbreaking stuff. Prior to this time, nobody has been able to properly measure financial independence. I have even been told that it can't be measured. As if it is some amorphous idea that can't be monitored or observed. But that is all wrong. You absolutely can measure financial independence. The FI metric is a simple formula that makes it possible and I will prove it to you.

> *Don't ever let anyone tell you that financial independence cannot be measured. It can be.*
>
> *I will show you how.*

When you go to the doctor, she takes your blood pressure to see how healthy you are. Your BP is a good measurement of how well your heart and cardiovascular system is working. Think of FI as if it's your financial BP. It will tell you how financially healthy you are. Do you need a financial quadruple bypass? Or are you ready for a financial triathlon? If you don't have a metric, then you can't tell.

This metric takes into account your financial situation and gives you a single number to focus on. A number that indicates your financial well being. If you go to the doctor and she doesn't take your BP, then you should suspect something is wrong with her methods. Likewise, if you go to a financial planner and he doesn't calculate your FI, you should think that something is wrong with his methods. But this is the norm for the time being. I am the only financial planner measuring FI today. I hope to change that. I hope to make the use of the FI metric wide spread and standard. Everyone should use it.

But the FI metric is more than just an informational tool. It's also a motivational tool. There is a philosophy that goes along with it. FI is a percentage that tells you how financially free you are. If your FI is 25, then you are 25% financially free. That also means that you are 75% wage slave. I hate being a wage slave. It bothers me. It's good motivation to work on increasing my FI. Hopefully, if *you* see that you are 75% wage slave, it will bother you too. Maybe it will give you some motivation to actually change your behaviors and decision making in order to improve your situation. To use the FI metric correctly, you have to get motivated and take action. You can't be passive. The metric is designed as a motivational tool **and** an informational tool.

What you want to do is to get your FI up to and over 100. If you accomplish that, then you are financially independent. What a powerful concept that is. A simple number that tells you everything you need to know about how your financial situation is progressing. You can throw out all the noise, all the garbage, all the narrative and just focus on that one single number. It is comprehensive. Nothing in your financial life will escape its view. It accounts for income, expenses, assets, liabilities, investment returns, credit card balances–everything. It is the perfect metric to put at the center of your financial life.

There is a lot going on in most people's financial lives. The FI metric is a way of turning off all of the chatter and getting down to what is really important to you. It's like a light beam that starts off wide and then narrows down to a single focused point. A laser beam focus. That's what the FI metric framework does. It puts your FI at the center of everything. Everything is done within the context of how it will affect your freedom–your FI. After all, this is your future we are talking about here. Shouldn't your freedom be at the center of planning for that future?

I came across a fabulous quotation regarding the future:

"When it comes to the future, there are three kinds of people; those who let it happen, those who make it happen, and those who wonder what happened "

~John M. Richardson Jr.

I just love that quote. I don't know what Mr. Richardson was thinking of when he wrote it, but it sure fits personal finances to a T. Let it happen, wonder what happened or make it happen. Those are your choices. Your future is coming one way or another.

I use a financial intensity scale that has three stereotypes. The "*let it happen*" people are like pawns. They kind of get pushed around by life. They just go with the flow and keep moving on down the road. They drift aimlessly wherever life leads them. Next we have the "*wonder what happened*" people. These folks are like drones. They get a plan of action in place, follow it for a long period of time and then get to the end of the journey and realize the plan they followed was no good. Finally, the "*make it happen*" people are like gladiators. They get thrown into an arena to fight for their life and they find a way to win. They know the consequences if they lose and they find it unacceptable to "*let it happen*" or to "*wonder what happened*" if they fail. Pawns, Drones, and Gladiators. They see the future differently and their perspectives are self fulfilling. When it comes to financial planning, the way you see the future will determine how you act today. And how you act today will determine what your future holds.

Pawns just "let it happen." Don't be a pawn.

Pawns are people who could summarize their plan as "I don't have a plan." They just go through life oblivious to the fact that there is a train wreck in their future. Pawns live paycheck to paycheck. Pawns are the people who will end up being entirely dependent on the government for their income. Pawns are the people who you will see at the payday loan store paying 300% interest so that they can have their money today instead of next week. They solve today's problem with no regard for tomorrow. A pawn's primary hopes of becoming financially independent are to win the lottery, sue somebody or see rich Uncle Fred kick the bucket sooner rather than later.

In today's financial environment, pawns are bound for a dismal future. Today, people are largely left to tend to their own financial future. The days of the golden watch and the fat pension are pretty much gone. If you don't have a plan for your financial future, then you won't like the results. Finances do not take care of themselves. The natural state, the path of least resistance, is poverty. If you don't do something, that is where you will end up. You have to take action to overcome that result. It won't happen by itself. You don't want to be a pawn.

Drones "wonder what happened." Don't be a drone.

Drones are next on the scale. Drones are people who are programmed to accomplish some task. They don't adapt. They don't question anything. They just follow their program and whatever happens, happens. Drones represent the current state of the financial planning industry. You might call them financial Yuppies. They hear an expert talk and they say, "Yup, sounds right to me". These are the folks who save 5% or 15% of their income in their 401(k) because some expert told them to do so. And they feel good about it. Drones are focused on some long-term target that is decades off into the future. They put away a small portion of their income because it makes them feel like they are doing the right thing. But they don't really understand their financial situation. They don't really know how dependent they are on their paychecks. They trust in the system. But they are letting time slip by and are making slow, minimal progress toward real financial freedom.

Drones are often well educated. They feel comfortable in their well-paying jobs. They read a few books on financial planning. They listen to Suze Orman and they watch CNBC. They pick a plan from their favorite financial expert, go on autopilot for 40 years and then crash into a wall and wonder how they got there. "*After all,*" they say, "*I was following a plan. I'm educated. I'm a professional. How did I end up this way?*" Yes, drones are following a plan. The problem is that they are following a really stupid plan. A plan that doesn't tell them where they stand. A plan that doesn't adapt. A plan that takes too long. A plan that is not aggressive enough. They have been sold a false bill of goods. They are told that they can spend, spend, spend, ignore their balance sheets, and save a fixed percentage of their income and everything will work out fine. They are told this because their financial planners don't have the courage to tell them how hard it really is to become financially independent. They don't have the courage to tell their client that they are headed for a dismal future. So, instead, they give their clients some watered down, user friendly plan that the client can live with. A plan that makes the client feel comfortable. Worst of all, the drones will find out that their plan is flawed when it is too late to do anything about it. Those poor little drones.

Gladiators "make it happen." Be a gladiator.

Finally, we have the gladiators. These are the folks who are ready to get serious. A gladiator is someone who knows he is a wage slave and just can't stand it. Gladiators don't want to spend one extra day in that state. They fight for their freedom and they use every tool available to them. They are focused on one thing and one thing only—their freedom. Everything else is secondary to that. Once they have their freedom, they can do great things. They can become financial anchors for their families. They can donate their time to charity. They can start businesses. They can live their dreams. But until that day comes, they are focused on that one main goal—Financial independence.

A gladiator will not blindly trust in the system. He wants to know the truth. Even if that truth is hard to face. He wants to know exactly where he stands. He does not want somebody's opinion about his financial situation. He wants proof. He works with facts so that he knows how much work he needs to do to reach his goal.

A gladiator does not exclude any viable method that will increase his freedom. IRAs and 401(k)s are great, but they are not the whole ball game. A gladiator invests in stocks, bonds, real estate, business or anything else that has a good risk-to-return ratio. He will work extra hours or a second job or start his own business to bolster his income in order to have more to invest. He will get degrees or credentials to help increase his earnings potential. He will cut expenses wherever possible. Everything is on the table for a gladiator.

Pawns, drones and gladiators. Everyone fits into one of those financial stereotypes. The FI metric framework can be used by anyone. But it is ideally suited for the gladiator mindset. It's for people who realize freedom has a price. It's for people who realize that the most valuable asset we have is time. And being forced to trade your time for money is a sad thing. If you are already a gladiator, then this system is for you. It will fit like a glove and you will excel at it. If you are a pawn or a drone, then you will find the system challenging because you will have to face the truth. The FI metric system will report to you every single month just how far off from success you are and how much work needs to be done. If you are not serious about it, then you won't like looking at it. The system is ruthlessly honest, so if you are on a bad path, it will tell you so. If you aren't willing to make changes, then you are not going to like what the framework has to tell you.

The FI metric framework is creative, unique and focused. There are two main parts to it. The first part is the mathematical part. The second part is the motivational part. The metric will allow you to stay on top of your financial health like never before. It's really the silver bullet of personal financial planning. Information and motivation both tied into the same metric. After you see the plan in action, you will agree that conventional planning is totally backwards. Conventional planning starts at the finish line and works its way back to the present day. The FI metric system starts with the here and now and works toward the finish line. It adjusts itself every single month based on your current financials.

The timing for this new approach is just perfect. Here in the U.S. we have gone through a major financial crisis. One of the worst in our country's history. The global economy has been shaken by too much debt and too lax standards. Lots of folks have been hurt in the process.

Virtually nobody has emerged unscathed in one way or another. On the bright side, it's like a forced spring cleaning has just occurred. Some folks are going to have to start over. Others are going to have to start a few steps back from where they were years ago. What better time than now to get a new plan in place to start working on your financial freedom. I can't guarantee that you will become financially free. But I can absolutely guarantee that you will not find a better framework to help you measure, monitor and improve your financial independence. You won't get this perspective from anyone else anywhere. It's all new and totally unique.

The framework is really simple. It works as follows. Every month, you will update your most important financial information. This information will be used to compute your FI. Your current financial independence level. After getting all of this information together, you will conduct a monthly meeting. During the meeting you will review the results from last month to see how you did. You will analyze your current situation and come up with possible strategies to use for the next month. Then, you will formalize those strategies in a plan of execution for the upcoming month. Finally, you will commit to the plan and begin execution. The month will go by and you will repeat the cycle.

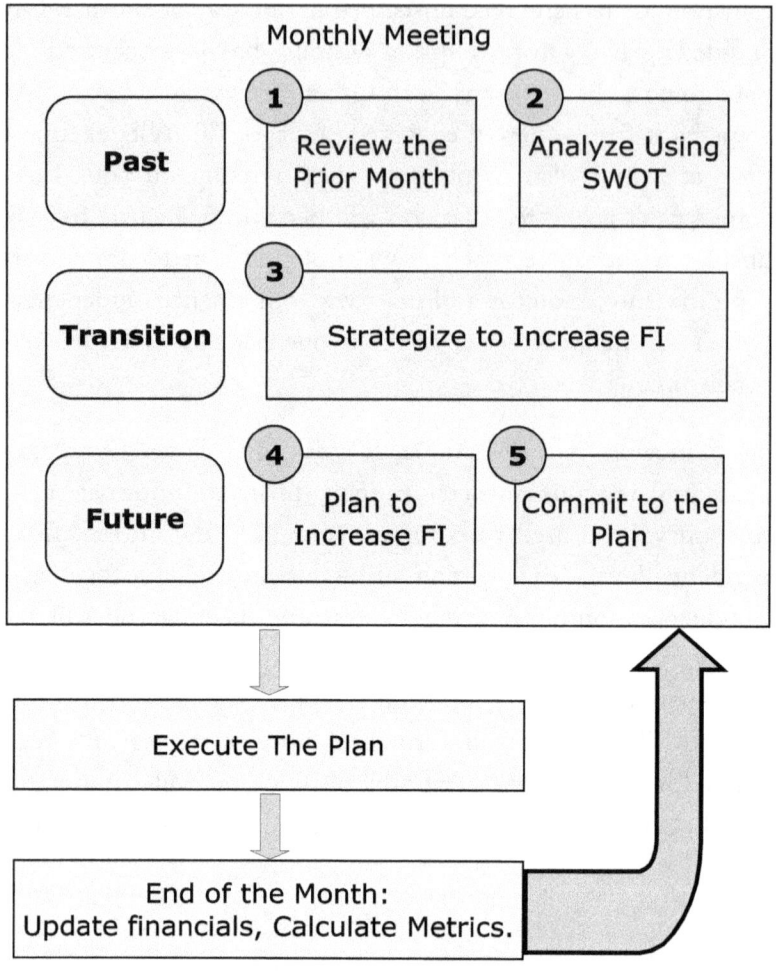

The key to the framework is that it will give you an accurate measurement of where you stand. The FI metric not only tells you how healthy your finances are, it will also work on your mental outlook to encourage behavioral changes. All of this is designed to put you on the right path to become financially independent as soon as possible. The FI metric is the centerpiece of the framework, so we will spend several chapters going over it.

Since the framework involves some computational math, it's not something that you are going to want to do without the help of a computer. You should find the formulas and the discussion of how they work to be very interesting, but you don't want to have to do this stuff by hand. Use the free tools on the FImetric website to compute your FI each month.

My hope is that the FI metric framework will catch on with folks all over the world. It fosters financial success and responsibility. It's as simple as possible but not simpler. It's just right for keeping you on the path to financial freedom. I hope you will give it a try. I hope you will see it for what it is. An honest system for personal financial success. Stick with it for a while and you will surely see improvements. Financial independence is extremely difficult to obtain. Good luck.

CHAPTER 1 KEYNOTES

1. Traditional financial planning is broken

2. You can measure financial independence

3. Don't let your future happen, make it happen

CHAPTER 2
FINANCIAL INDEPENDENCE

"Wealth is the ability to fully experience life."

~ Henry David Thoreau

Several years back I was giving a presentation at a local university. I stood up in front of a panel of professors and local business leaders and boldly told them that I had a way to measure financial independence. As expected, I got some backlash from some of them. One gentleman in particular told me that I could not possibly measure financial independence. He said financial independence means something different for one person than it is does for another. He was wrong. In this chapter, I will lay the foundation to explain why.

This is the beginning of the process of measuring FI. But to measure it, we need a good definition for it. Let's put together a crystal clear definition of just what it means to be financially independent. It will only take one short sentence to do it.

First off, let me clarify the difference between the terms subjective and objective. Subjective means what a particular person is thinking. Subjective thoughts are tainted by a person's experiences, beliefs and perspectives. Subjective thoughts can't be verified. They are the opinion of the speaker. Objective, on the other hand, means what a reasonable person would think by looking at the facts. Objective is unbiased and verifiable. Obviously, if we want a good definition for financial independence, we should try for objectivity.

Financial independence is not the same as terms like "rich" or "wealthy" or "well off." Those terms are clearly subjective. They mean different things to different people. We can't verify them. What Bill Gates or Mark Zuckerberg consider "rich" may be quite different from what you or I consider "rich." Likewise, what Warren Buffet considers "wealthy" is probably not the same as what I consider "wealthy." Financial independence is different. It is objective, not subjective. We can take an unbiased look at someone's financial situation and decide if that person is financially independent or not. It is fact, not opinion. It is verifiable based upon the numbers.

So, in order to determine someone's financial independence, we have to get a clear picture of two things. We need to know about their financial situation **and** about their lifestyle. We can't look solely at their income. Nor can we look solely at their assets and liabilities. We need to know how their behaviors and habits are impacting their financial situation as well. Consider Mike Tyson, Willie Nelson, Ed McMahon and many others who have earned millions and millions of dollars but have squandered it all away. If we look at their outrageous incomes we may falsely conclude that they are financially independent. If we look at their balance sheets, we will realize they are financial idiots. They have lived undisciplined financial lives and have squandered away their incomes. We need a way to tie together income, net worth and lifestyle. They are all components of financial independence.

Think about the words themselves–"Financial Independence." They are actually very clear. To be financially *independent* means that we are not financially *dependent*. I think we can universally agree that what we are trying to become independent of is our jobs. In other words, we don't want to have to sacrifice our time to meet our financial needs. Time is the most precious asset we have. We don't want to be "dependent" upon the giving up of our time in exchange for money in order to maintain our lifestyle. We don't want to be dependent on our paychecks. What we want is to be able to rely on something else to generate our income for us. We want to rely on financial resources that do not require us to sacrifice our time. We could use stocks, bonds, rental real estate, or a passive business. The main criteria is that we don't want to be forced to give up our time in order for those resources to work for us.

Given this discussion, I will define financial independence as follows:

"The ability to maintain one's lifestyle without relying on time-based income"

There, that wasn't so difficult. That definition is simple, clear, and completely in line with what the vast majority of people would mean when they really think about the term. Notice how precise the definition is. There is no subjectivity involved at all. It is totally objective in nature. The reason it's objective is because it considers both financial resources and lifestyle. Live a lavish lifestyle and you will require more resources. Live a modest lifestyle and you will require fewer resources. Financial independence is measured appropriately in both cases.

Maybe someday I will find that definition in the back of one of those financial planning textbooks. It should be there. It should be in every book about personal finances and financial independence. It would have been so easy for those folks to put that one critical definition in their glossary. For now, you and I can live out here on the cutting edge and wait for the experts to catch up with us. Congratulations, you are already ahead of our renowned financial experts.

The idea here is to shift your financial dependence away from time-based income and toward other resources. We don't care too much what those resources are as long as they don't require our time. You may use stocks, bonds, real estate, passive business, pension payments, annuities or other financial instruments. The best case is a well diversified collection of such resources. We are always financially dependent on something or someone. What we refer to as financial independence is that we are not dependent on sacrificing our *time* in order to maintain our lifestyle.

There is a financial instrument called a lifetime annuity which pays out recurring payments for a person's remaining life. Let's say I give you a lifetime annuity that is adjusted to keep up with inflation. This annuity starts off paying you $10,000 a month and then increases each year for inflation and will keep paying you for the rest of your life. That's a pretty sweet deal for you. But does it make you financially independent? We can't tell. We are still missing half of the equation. We are missing the important component of knowing what your lifestyle is like. Are you spending like one of the "Housewives of Orange County" or are you living like a frugal monk? Are you investing some of that $10K per month? How are those investments doing? Are you taking on debt? How much is the interest costing you? We can't determine if you are financially independent because we simply don't have enough information. If the $10K per month adjusted for inflation is enough to maintain your lifestyle, then yes, you are financially independent. If your lifestyle is beyond the means of the annuity payments, then you are not.

So, let's say that you decide to set aside some of the $10K each month and live on about $8K. Well then you are 100% financially independent. The annuity pays for your lifestyle **and** your net worth is increasing each month. There is no need for you to sacrifice your time for money. You can work if you choose to, but you are not forced to do so. And, if you do decide to work, you can work in whatever field you would like to. Your decision need not be driven by money. If we calculated the FI metric for you, we would find that it is greater than 100.

On the other hand, let's suppose that you decide $10K is a lot of money so you want to get a new Ferrari. And you want to rent a luxury home. And with that kind of income, you certainly need a nice wardrobe. Your expenses are running at $20K per month. Since your annuity only covers $10K, where will you get the other half? Same place that all wage slaves get it. You will go back to work because you are not financially independent. In this case you are approximately 10/20=50% financially independent. If we calculated your FI, we would find that it is somewhere around 50.

That's the general idea behind the FI metric. Consider your lifestyle and your financial resources and calculate how financially free you are. The metric doesn't actually use the calculation as shown here. It's a bit more complicated. But the underlying idea is the same. Here, I am using expenses to determine what your lifestyle is like. The FI metric formula uses something more powerful than expenses. We will get to that in the next chapter. I'm just keeping things simple for now for the sake of argument.

I just gave you two scenarios. Both with the same income source—the $10K per month annuity. In the first case you lived within the means of your financial resources. In the second case you did not. In both cases, we are easily able to determine if you are financially independent or not. We don't have to guess about your financial independence level in the two cases. We just look at the facts and determine financial independence based on the numbers. It's not opinion, it's fact. It's verifiable. You've either got it or you don't. An eighth grader could look at those two scenarios and tell us which reflects financial independence.

Remember the story I told you about when I did the presentation in front of the college panel? I told them I could measure financial independence and one of the panel members argued that I couldn't do that because financial independence meant something different to each person. Well, so much for that argument. It just went out the window. That argument would have held water if I were talking about terms like "rich" or "wealthy." But it's completely wrong when we talk about the term financial independence. I can't measure "wealthy." I can't measure "rich." But I damn well can measure financial independence. Given my definition of financial independence, you can see that it is not open to interpretation, opinion or bias. Look at it again:

"The ability to maintain one's lifestyle without relying on time-based income".

With this as my definition, it's clear that financial independence is an unbiased objective look at one's financial situation. We can take a fair look at a person's financial information, along with their lifestyle, and we can determine how financially independent they are.

This definition makes it clear that financial independence is not about being rich or wealthy. It's about freedom. It's about being in control of your time. There is nothing in that definition about having a certain amount of wealth, or having a certain amount of stuff. It's all about having control of your time. Adjust your lifestyle and adjust your financial resources such that you are not dependent on sacrificing your time to earn money. That's what financial independence is all about.

I'm not really sure why some people push back against the idea of being able to measure financial independence. Yeah, it's a new idea, but if you open your mind and think about it, it makes perfect sense. In the financial world, we use metrics every day. There are lots of financial metrics out there–return on investment (ROI), return on equity (ROE), price earnings ratio (PE), risk-adjusted return on capital (RAROC). Heck the Dow Jones, S&P 500 and Nasdaq are just metrics for how the stock market is doing. Millions of people use those metrics every day. Financial metrics like those are widely used and widely accepted as credible. They are all objective measurements. They are computed with simple formulas. Financial independence is just like those other metrics. There is absolutely no reason why we cannot measure it given the correct formula. I'll be giving you that formula in the next few chapters. That doubting Thomas college professor was familiar with some of those financial metrics. He knew about PE and ROI. He accepts those as valid metrics. There is no reason why he should not accept the fact that I can create a metric for financial independence. Well, no reason other than he had a closed mind. Open your mind and follow along with me as I show you how this new metric works. Yes, financial independence can be measured. Don't let anyone tell you that you can't measure it. You can and you must.

The measurement applies for any person regardless of current income level or position. If a person is willing to give us his or her personal financial information, then we can determine if that person is financially independent or not. It applies to fast food workers, janitors, doctors, lawyers, celebrities, business tycoons—everyone. It doesn't discriminate in its application. It doesn't care what your profession is. It doesn't care what your attitude is. It doesn't care if you are Gordon Gekko or Mahatma Gandhi. Punch in the numbers, spit out the result. You are either financially independent or you are not. The numbers decide. There is no opinion, bias or judgment involved.

Back when I was studying financial planning, I was taught that the very first thing I should do with my clients was to establish goals. I think that makes a lot of sense. Studies show that if you establish goals, you are far more likely to succeed. I was also taught that it is up to the client to establish his goals. But I disagree with that approach. I'm not going to ask you what your goal is, I'm going to TELL you what it should be.

Your goal should be to become financially independent. It should not be to retire, or to become a millionaire, or to save for your kids' education. It should be to become financially independent. All other goals are secondary.

> *I'm not going to ask you what your goal is. I'm going to TELL you what it should be. Your goal should be to become financially independent as soon as possible.*

Why such a hard line on this one goal? Because it is the right thing to do. It is the responsible thing to do. What business do we have planning for other things when we have not met up to our responsibility to provide for our own financial needs. Some people may think that it is greedy to want to be financially independent. In fact, it's just the opposite. If you are working on other goals, then YOU are the one who is being greedy. Because if you are working on some other goal and you lose your job, then you become a burden on everyone else. Your family, your community, your fellow taxpayers. They all have to chip in to support you because you did not provide for own financial independence. Get this done first and then you can set other goals.

I know that there are people out there who will say, "No, I will sacrifice my financial independence in order to save for my child's education." Well, how noble you must feel. But this is just weakness disguised as nobility. In the long run, you will hurt yourself and your child. Who is going to help their child more over their lifetime? The guy who goes into debt to pay for his kids' education? Or the guy who gets tough and becomes financially independent? I would argue that the financially independent guy is going to do far more for his child over his lifetime than the guy who reaches out to help now when he is really in no position to offer that help. You may get sick, or injured or laid off, and then you will become a burden to your children. They will have to pay for you for the rest of your life. Your good intentions will lead to a bad result. Take care of your own financial independence first. Build a solid base and then you can go out and help others or target different goals of your own.

Another reason that I am taking a hard line on making financial independence your goal is that if I left it to you, you may likely pick a bad goal. It's all the rage now to try to become debt free. Many folks are making that their number one goal. But think about it. Is debt free really a good goal? A newborn baby enters the world debt free. Does it make sense to make it your goal to get to the same financial position as a newborn baby? Of course not. What happens when you finally reach your goal of becoming debt free? Answer, nothing. You'll still have to hop into your car and drive to work the next day. Debt free is fine as a sub goal, but as a main goal it sucks. Financially independent is infinitely better than debt free. Debt free is not a life changer. Financial independence is. If you were an athlete training for the 100 meters in the Olympics and I was your coach, then you would probably think it pretty strange if I trained you on nothing but 10 meter sprints. We would look pretty silly jumping around celebrating because you are the world's fastest human being at 10 meters. What about the other 90? It's fine to train and make those first 10 meters as fast as you can. But don't forget about the rest of the race. Aiming for debt free as your main goal is like training for nothing but the first 10 meters. They are both ok as sub goals. But they are terrible as primary goals. Financial independence, that's what you need to shoot for.

What would the three different stereotypes think about my definition of financial independence? First off, the pawn. Well, chances are you couldn't get a pawn to sit down and pay attention long enough to even listen to the definition. If you could, it would go in one ear and out the other. Pawns have no plan. They think things will take care of themselves. So why would they care about financial independence. These are the folks who will become burdens to all of us. They will have financial needs even though they are not prepared for them. So the rest of society will have to pick up the tab for them. Am I being a little harsh on pawns? Yes, I am. They need a wakeup call. They need to hear the harshness. If someone doesn't tell them that they are headed for big trouble, then they are certain to find it.

What about you drones out there who have been faithfully saving 5% or 15% of your income in your 401(k)s? My definition of financial independence should make perfect sense to a drone. Sure, even drones would like to be in control of their time and not be forced to work every day in a particular job. But likely, a drone just absorbs the new definition and proceeds forward with the current plan, unaltered and unchanged. That's what drones do. They stay on target, they follow the plan. Regardless of how bad the plan is. What a drone *should* do is to consider how her current plan is really working out for her. Is her plan doing anything to increase her financial independence? Or is she just a hamster on the wheel going in circles and waiting for some big day decades into the future? The drones continue on their path, flying on blind faith. They are trusting in their plans to take care of them on some great day in the future. And when that day comes, will it really be what they had planned for or will there be some surprises for the poor little drones? Since their plans don't have a metric to check, I guess they will have to wait a few decades and find out when it happens.

Now, on to the real winners. The gladiators. The folks who are willing to do what it takes to win at this game. The gladiator meditates on this definition of financial independence:

"The ability to maintain one's lifestyle without relying on time-based income".

After considering it, the gladiator says "Hell Yeah! That's what I want. I want to live my life and take control of my time." To the financial gladiator, dependence on time-based income is evil. It is the binding of slavery. It is something to be eradicated. You don't wait for it to happen. You don't trust in the plan to take care of it. While a drone may be able to live with a 40 or 50 year plan to reduce his dependence on time based income, a gladiator simply can't accept that. He says to himself, "What, I'm going to sit here in my sorry wage slave state and just take this garbage for 40 years. I don't think so. I have a life to live and I don't plan on living it under the control of somebody else. I'm ready to attack this problem head on. Let's go!" Now that is someone who is ready for freedom planning. That is somebody who is ready for the FI metric.

Bob Dylan has a famous quote that says

"What's money? A man is a success if he gets up in the morning and goes to bed at night and in between does what he wants to do."

Bob has it partially right. When we are working on our financial independence, it's not because we are all caught up in money. It's not because we are greedy. It's because we want to control what we do from when we get up in the morning until we go to bed. Simply put, we want freedom. On the other hand, for most of us the reality is that money is very important. We are not so fortunate to get to do something that we love to do and get paid for it. We have obligations to meet. People to provide for. We can't just pick up a guitar and sing all day like Bob does. So, we face up to our obligations and we sacrifice our time to earn money. Even if it means doing something that we don't really want to do. We roll out of bed and slog off to work because we are responsible and because we want to provide for the people that we love and care for.

This is a paradox of sorts. Money is not what is important to us. What we really want is freedom. But to get that, we need enough money to maintain a standard of living. So, money becomes important to us. For a financial gladiator, money is just a tool. It is a means to an end. If you use it to fulfill every indulgence under the sun and you still can't get enough, then you are clearly greedy. If you use it to earn your freedom, then you are using it wisely. You are putting the tool to good use.

How dependent are you on your own time-based income right now? Are you a pawn? Will you just remain oblivious to the fact that the best hours of your life are being spent for the benefit of your employer? Will you miss out on time with your family because you have to exchange that time for money? Will you spend your entire life dependent on someone else?

Maybe you are a drone. Is your plan good enough to rid you of your dependence on time based income? How long will you wait to find out? Ten years, twenty, fifty maybe? Or have you faced the truth? Have you realized the fact that you are dependent on sacrificing your time for money to meet your lifestyle demands? Have you become a gladiator? The gladiator may have to drag himself out of bed every morning and slog off to make a living just like the pawn and the drone, but he does so with purpose. He does so with focus. He does so with the intent that he will do this for as short a time as possible and then he will be free. He is unwilling to wait decades for this to happen. He fights for it every day.

CHAPTER 2 KEYNOTES

1. We can define financial independence

2. Financial Independence is about freedom

3. Debt free is not a good primary goal

4. Your goal should be financial independence

CHAPTER 3
EQUITY GROWTH

"Those who expect to reap the blessings of freedom must, like men, undergo the fatigue of supporting it."

~ Thomas Paine

Dependence on time based income (TBI) is the financial gladiator's worst enemy. He will do anything to stomp it out. If we want our freedom back, then we need to rid ourselves of our dependence on TBI. Because it is that very dependence that robs us of our time and freedom. It steals our youth and takes us away from our family, friends and interests. But if you want to get rid of TBI, then you need something to stand in its place. That something is equity growth. Equity growth is what can ultimately provide financial independence. It is your best weapon against being dependent on TBI. The focus of this book is the FI metric. If equity growth weren't a major component of FI, then you should suspect that there is a major problem. Of course, that is not the case. Equity growth is a key component of the FI metric. That makes perfect sense because the fuel that feeds financial freedom is equity growth.

What is equity? Some people think that equity only exists in homes. Not true. Actually, equity is an accounting term that denotes ownership. Equity can exist in lots of things. You have equity in your savings account. You have equity in your 401(k). You have equity in your automobiles. To determine equity, you use a financial statement called the balance sheet. Equity is used as the bottom line number of a balance sheet. On a balance sheet, equity represents all that is left over after creditors have made their claims against assets. The balance sheet, and its calculation of equity, are necessities for computing FI. So let's spend some time going over the balance sheet in detail.

A balance sheet is a like a snapshot of your finances. It says what your financial condition is as of some moment in time. Like taking a picture and freezing that moment so that it can be analyzed and reviewed. In fact, the balance sheet is also referred to as the statement of financial position. Think of it as taking into account all of the things that have ever happened in your financial life and showing the end result of all of that activity. It's a powerful financial statement which conveys a lot of good information.

The best news of all is that it is really simple to create a balance sheet. Start off by listing all of your assets. Assets are all of the things that you own. Things that have significant financial value. For a personal balance sheet, assets would include things like:

Primary Residence
Retirement Accounts (401(k)s, IRAs, etc.)
Bonds
Stocks
Savings Accounts
Certificates of Deposit
Rental Property
Annuities
Cash Value Life Insurance
Cars

In general, I would leave off things like low-end consumer electronics and other personal items. Even though they may have value, they generally lose their value so quickly that they are really not worth tracking on your balance sheet. You can track them if you want to, but it's just simpler to admit that their effective value is probably going to be zero very quickly. I'm not opposed to tracking them. For one thing, it will make it clear to you what a terrible investment they are. They will drop in value month after month until they become worthless. I just think it's clear to most people that such assets are essentially worthless after purchase so it's not worth taking the time to track them. Now, if you have some high-end expensive item like a $25,000 home theater projector, then yes, by all means track it. If you wanted to sell it, you could probably get a chunk of dough for it. So it is an asset worth tracking. Use your judgment for each of your assets and decide on your own.

Before I move on to the rest of the balance sheet, let me talk about a pet peeve of mine. I often hear financial advisors tell people to exclude their residence when they are looking at their financial assets. That may be one of the dumbest things that I have ever heard. Why in the world would you exclude one of your largest assets from your financial statement? Are you just supposed to act like it's not there? For the life of me, I can't think of a single justification for ignoring your residence. It's an asset and it should be included. If you own a house with $1 million in equity and someone else is just a renter, then there is a real financial difference there. You can't ignore it. These folks try to justify this stupid guideline by saying that you can't "spend" your house. Well, if you have a home that really has $1 million in equity then all you have to do to spend it is to sell it. Duh! Ignore such moronic advice and include your home as an asset on your balance sheet.

I have also heard some financial advisors butcher the meaning of the term asset. I heard one famous advisor saying if real estate does not produce positive cash flow then it is not an asset, it's a liability. I won't say who he the advisor was, but he has two dads. One is well off and the other is not. Anyway, this guy said that if a house has negative cash flow then it's a liability. I say he is financially illiterate! When it comes to balance sheet classification, it makes no difference if your real estate produces positive cash flow or not. It's a thing of significant value so it's an asset. Not all assets are good. Cars are assets. They are bad assets, but assets nonetheless. They have significant value. That value goes down month after month, so they are not the kind of assets we prefer, but they are still assets.

Some of your assets have an obvious value. Banking and investment accounts generally have actual dollar amounts for them. These are easy to value on your balance sheet. Other assets take just a little bit more work. In the past it was somewhat difficult to get an estimate of the value of your home or your car. But nowadays the internet makes it really easy to get a good estimated value for most of your assets. Need the value of your house this month? Just go to www.zillow.com and you can get a reasonable estimate. Need the value of your car? Go to Kelley Blue Book at www.kbb.com and you can get a good idea of what it is currently worth. Adjust those estimates as needed so that you can get a realistic idea of the value for each of your assets. It doesn't have to be perfect, just as accurate as you can reasonably be. Be consistent and make your best guess. Once you have listed out all of your assets, total them up and you will have total assets.

Next, list out all of your liabilities. No, I'm not talking about your ex-wife. Liabilities are your creditor's claims against your assets. They are things that you owe to others. These would include all of the following:

Mortgages
Car Loans
Credit Card Balances
Personal Loans
Student Loans

Once you have all of your liabilities listed, total them up to get your total liabilities.

Finally, you need to compute your net worth—or equity. To compute equity, just subtract total liabilities from total assets. Net worth and equity are the same thing. I prefer the term equity so that is what I will use from now on. But, keep in mind that they mean the same thing. It's just assets minus liabilities.

This is why the statement is called a balance sheet. There are two parts to it. In part one, you have all of the assets. In part 2, you have all of the claims against those assets. The claims that are for creditors are called liabilities. The claims that are yours are called equity. You get whatever's left over after your creditors are covered. Liabilities and equity must total to equal the total amount of assets. It is always in balance.

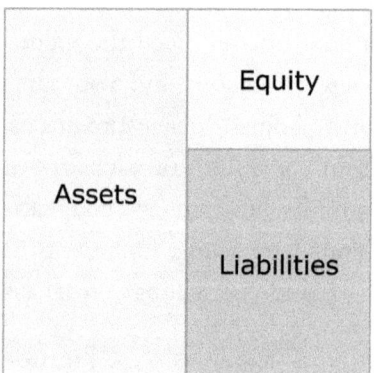

For many folks, creating a balance sheet should be quick work. You could probably get it done in less than half an hour. And, once you have it laid out, it should be even quicker to update it with current values. A typical balance sheet might look like this:

```
                    BALANCE SHEET
                JACK AND DIANE SMITH
                   MARCH 31, 2011

Primary Residence                           $330,000.00
Rental Property on E Street                 $175,000.00
Jack's 401(k)                               $115,000.00
Diane's 401(k)                               $46,250.00
Scottrade Investment Account                 $32,000.00
Chase Savings Account                        $13,000.00
2009 Honda Accord                            $12,850.00
TOTAL ASSETS                                $724,000.00

Primary Mortgage                            $240,000.00
Rental Mortgage                             $124,250.00
Mastercard Balance                            $3,250.00
Visa Balance                                  $4,800.00
Jack's Student Loan                          $16,800.00
Auto Loan - Accord                           $14,500.00
TOTAL LIABILITIES                           $403,600.00

EQUITY                                        $320,500
```

Nothing complicated here, just list out your financial assets and liabilities in order to see where you stand on things. Make sure that your equity is calculated as assets minus liabilities and you are set.

Balance sheets are great financial tools. They let you know what your current financial position is. Even if you didn't have the FI metric system to follow, I would recommend preparing a balance sheet on a regular basis to make sure you know where you stand on your assets and liabilities.

What we are after for the FI metric is monitoring the change in your equity over time. To get that, just create a balance sheet at the end of each month. Then, subtract last month's equity from this month's equity to get your change in equity. Change in equity is a critical measurement. I can't believe how rarely I see it discussed by financial advisors. I've read tons of books on personal finance. I watch shows on personal finance. And I don't ever remember hearing anyone talk about equity growth. What are they thinking? Equity growth is critical. It's really the whole ball game.

Equity growth is the fuel of financial freedom. Monitor it every month. The more equity growth you have, the more freedom you have.

Equity growth is what you want to see. The more, the better. If your equity goes up that's good. If it's flat or going down, that's bad. If you want to know if you are making progress from one month to the next, then equity growth is what you should look at.

Equity growth occurs in one of two ways. First, you get equity growth when you pay off debt. When you pay off debt, your liabilities go down and your equity goes up. Also, you get equity growth when your assets increase in value. If your assets increase without a corresponding increase in liabilities, then your equity must increase.

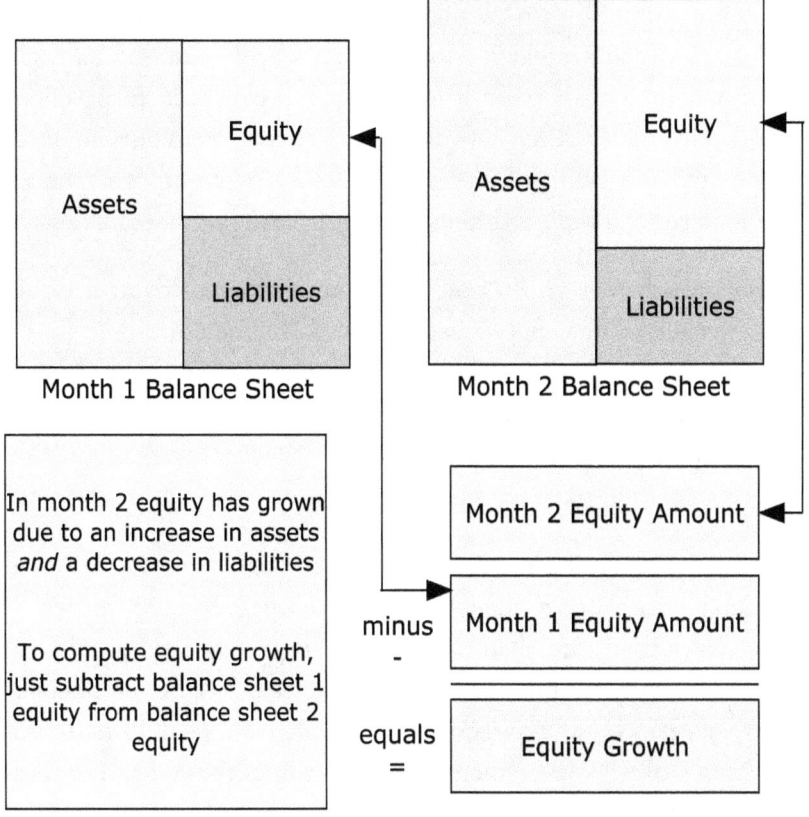

Increases to assets occur in two ways. First, you can invest new money. This is what happens with your 401(k) account. You put in new money every paycheck so your asset increases and your equity increases accordingly. The second way to increase assets is investment return. You have invested in the past and those investments increase in value (hopefully). So your assets increase in value and your equity grows.

Ideally, you want to attack your equity growth from both sides. Do whatever you can to pay off your debts and also do whatever you can to increase your assets. Pay off debt, invest new money, and get good investment returns. These are the things that lead to equity growth.

If you are working your tail off every month and your equity is not increasing, then you are like a hamster on a wheel. Working hard and getting nowhere. This is what it means to live paycheck to paycheck. You work all month, receive your check and pay for your expenses. Then you start the next month right where you were before. You are on the financial treadmill. Working hard and getting nowhere.

Equity growth tells you if you are making progress or not. Equity growth is critical to financial success and it should be monitored. In the FI metric plan, you will compute it in order to get an even more important metric. The FI metric. That's where we are headed. But it is important to note the significance of equity growth itself. Any quality financial plan should track equity growth.

How many books have you read on personal finances? I've read lots. I don't remember a single one that discussed equity growth. I certainly never read one that stressed the importance of monitoring equity growth every month. As you can see, it's a basic component of financial success. How can any financial plan succeed if it doesn't monitor this critical measurement? And yet, this is the norm. If you go to a financial planner today, I bet you he won't send you away with a plan that tells you to measure your equity growth every month. He should, but he won't.

You'll find lots of books that talk about budgeting and expense tracking. But those things are of lesser importance to equity. If you monitor your equity, then you are already monitoring your expenses. It's just that you are cutting out all the background noise. Who cares about every little tiny expense that you make. What matters is the end result. And the measurement for that is equity growth. If your equity is growing rapidly, then your expenses are under control. If your equity is standing still or declining, then your expenses are out of control. I've got nothing against budgeting and expense tracking. But don't get a fancy budget and forget to measure your change in equity. That would be like counting every single calorie and never getting on the scale. The scale is what tells you if the calorie counting is working. Likewise, equity growth tells you if your budget is working.

Without looking at equity growth you don't know what kind of overall progress you are making. You won't know if you are spinning your wheels. And it's such an easy thing to do. It only takes a short amount of time to crank out a monthly balance sheet and compute your equity growth every month. Make a commitment to do this yourself every single month.

Let's run through our financial continuum and see how our three stereotypes view equity growth. We know pawns don't care about equity growth. If they had any equity, they would cash it out and spend it immediately. They can't see past this week, much less next year.

Drones don't do much better. They trust in their 401(k)'s. They trust in their 15% savings rate. They are happy to remain blind to what their balance sheet is telling them. It's probably too painful to look at. They take comfort in the growing balance in their retirement account, but they don't look at the growing liabilities that are racking up on their balance sheets. The drones have never heard of this idea of equity growth and using it as a substitute for time-based income. Likely, the drones are somewhat interested in this concept, but they will continue to put their faith in their current plan. It's more conventional and seems more prudent. Suze has never talked to them about equity growth. So it can't be very important. The truth is that the drone is following a plan that encourages ignorance of the facts. It's ostrich mentality. Bury your head in the sand and ignore reality. Come on, drones, pull your head out and see the light.

The gladiator is on the complete opposite end of the spectrum. She can't wait until the end of each month to find out how much equity growth she has accomplished. She looks forward to seeing her equity growth increase more and more each month. She knows that if she wants to take control of her time, equity growth is the tool to accomplish it. It is the sword which will hack through the chains of her bondage. It is the thing that will eradicate her dependence on time-based income. The gladiator finds ways to increase equity growth every single month. If she had $X worth of equity growth last month, then she wants $X+[something more] for this month.

CHAPTER 3 KEYNOTES

1. Dependence on TBI is your enemy

2. Complete a balances sheet every month

3. Measure your equity growth and understand its importance

4. Equity growth can act as a substitute for TBI

CHAPTER 4
THE FI METRIC

"None are so hopelessly enslaved as those who falsely believe they are free."

~ Goethe

A while back, I was very interested in flying. So I went through flight school and earned my pilot's license. I found out that one of the leading causes of general aviation accidents was running out of fuel. Can you believe that? All of the preparation and safety steps that you take and then you freakin run out of fuel! Imagine the scene as two guys are flying across country: rrrrrrrr ... cough, cough... "Hey Fred, the engine is cutting out–what's going on here? Oh Geez, I'm really sorry Joe, it looks like I forgot to fill the tank. It's been nice knowing you. We're going doooown." I'd strangle that sucker before we hit the ground.

Metrics are important. A fuel gauge makes for a nice metric in an airplane. It's one thing to have a metric. It's another thing to have the right metric. We smart pilots don't trust our lives to gauges. We actually open the tank and look at the fuel level ourselves before takeoff. For flying airplanes, that's the right metric.

Crazy as it sounds, conventional financial planning is a lot like flying without checking your fuel tanks. There is a lot of blind faith involved. The typical financial planning process will involve doing some elaborate calculations about values way into the future. Then, the results are analyzed using some prudent sounding rules of thumb. This analysis will lead to calculating what you should be doing now. And then, a wave of the magic wand happens and you will just be told to save 10% or 15% of your income. It's amazing that no matter how detailed the forward looking projection is, they always just come back and settle on 10%, 15% or 20%. How come it never comes out to 18% or 39%? What does that tell you about the real quality of the process that they are using? If their process was good, then they wouldn't just round off to the nearest 5%. Those few percentage points can make a huge difference over time. Financial planners round off to the nearest 5% because it's easy. It sounds good. And their plan is just a bunch of guess work anyway so why not. They run some calculations to make themselves look smart and then somehow they just shoehorn it back into a fixed savings rate of 15% or 20%. And after all of this, you part ways with your planner and go on autopilot for years and years to wait and see what happens. Sounds a lot like flying without knowing how much fuel you have in your tank to me. Traditional planning is weak when it comes to metrics. But the FI metric system is completely centered around the most important metric of all. How much freedom you have.

The FI metric is the financial version of opening up the tank and checking the fuel level. You shouldn't trust your life to a fuel gauge and you shouldn't trust your financial freedom to a plan with no metric. If you wake up one day when you are 65 or 70 years old and find out that your finances are a wreck, you may want to strangle your financial advisor just like I would strangle an irresponsible pilot who risks my life over a lazy mistake. But you won't be able to blame me, because I am giving you the perfect system to allow you to monitor your finances. Good or bad, you will know exactly how much financial fuel you have in your tank. Now, let's go through the steps to derive the FI metric.

> *You shouldn't trust your financial freedom to a plan with no metric. The FI metric system is all about monitoring your financial freedom.*

Here is my definition of financial independence one more time.

Financial Independence: "The ability to maintain one's lifestyle without relying on time-based income".

There are two major parts to that definition. Time-based Income (TBI) and lifestyle. To get a metric for FI, we need to cover both of those components. As we learned in the last chapter, equity growth is what we will use as a substitute for time-based income. You already know how to measure equity growth. You just need two balance sheets. You subtract the equity on last month's balance sheet from this month's balance sheet and you have equity growth. Let's dial in the measurement of time-based income.

Measuring time-based income is easy. All we have to do is track our income and determine how much of it is based on sacrificing our time. This is the income that we don't want to rely on. If we have income from royalties, rents, annuities, passive business or investments that do not require us to sacrifice our time, then we are happy. But, if our income comes from sources that require us to sacrifice our time, then we are not so happy. Time-based income is income from your job.

Income from your paycheck. It's wage slave income. We need to reduce our dependency on such income as much as possible. So, to come up with time-based income, all you have to do is look at all of your current income sources and classify them as time based or non-time based. We are going to make all of these measurements on a monthly basis. At the end of each month, just add up the dollar amounts of all the income sources for which you had to sacrifice your time.

You may have some sources of income that are split. They require some time, but they are not completely dependent on your time. Just come up with a percentage estimate to use for such income. For example, I have royalties from some software that I wrote years ago, but I have to do some minimal maintenance on that software each year to get the royalties. So, I classify that income as 10% time-based. Come up with your own percentage if you have any similar income. Once you have come up with your percentage, just apply it to that source to split it up into time based and non-time based.

Track your TBI after taxes. Not your net check, but your gross minus taxes. If you have other things taken out of your check like health insurance, 401(k) contributions or loan payments, then those things still need to be included. Just take the gross amount and subtract out all taxes including federal, state, local and payroll taxes. If you get perks like an employer matching contribution to your 401(k), then you need to add those things into your TBI. That should make sense because if you lost your paycheck, you would also lose that 401(k) employer contribution as well. TBI should represent the money that you would lose if you were to get rid of your paycheck.

For most people, this just means you have to go through your paycheck once and determine what your TBI is. For the vast majority of people, TBI will be the same every month since they get the same paycheck every month. Once you have it, you can keep using the same number unless something changes with your paycheck.

Now we have time-based income for the month and we have change in equity for the month. We need to combine them to come up with FI. Let's get fancy and make some mathematical terms for them.

TBI=Time-Based income

ΔE=Change in Equity

The Greek symbol Δ (delta) is used in mathematics to denote change. ΔE is pronounced (delta E) and it represents change in equity.

If we put these two terms together in just the right way, then we get the magic that we need. We get an accurate measurement of financial independence, the FI metric. Here is the formula in its simplified form:

$$FI = \frac{\Delta E}{TBI}$$

That's it. What this says is that financial independence is change in equity divided by time-based income. The relationship between change in equity and time based income tells us how financially independent we are. The reason that it works is that we want to use equity growth as a substitute for time based income. Equity growth acts like a proxy for your time-based income. It stands in its place. When equity growth is large enough, it can act as a complete replacement for TBI. If our change in equity is half of our time-based income, then we are only halfway to the goal. Or, we are 50% financially independent. Once our equity growth is greater than or equal to our time-based income, then we are financially independent. Well, sort of.

I wish the formula could stay as is, but we need to complicate it some. There are two other pesky things we need to deal with. Inflation and taxes. Before we move on to those things, just make sure that you understand why the formula works. It's really a very simple idea. It just says that there is no better way to determine how dependent you are on your time-based income than to look at what is really happening with your financial world. And, the best measurement for that is equity growth. So, to determine financial independence, we ask you to prove that you are not dependent on your time-based income by showing us that your equity is growing at least as fast as the amount of your time-based income. If your equity growth is at least as large as your TBI, then you could get rid of TBI and use your equity growth as a substitute. All of this is objective, unbiased and verifiable. We won't take your word for it and it is not open to opinion. We look at your finances and we come to a conclusion.

$$FI = \frac{\Delta E}{TBI}$$

Notice that the formula considers how much TBI you have *and* what you are doing with it. What you are doing with your TBI is reflected in equity growth. If you are a doctor or lawyer, then maybe you have a lot of TBI. If so, then in order to become financially independent, you better be seeing a lot of equity growth. The higher TBI is, the higher equity growth needs to be. Think of this formula as a demand of proof. It's saying that we won't believe you when you claim to be financially free. We require you to demonstrate it for us. You can demonstrate it for us by showing us that your equity growth is greater than your time-based income. We don't care what you claim. We care what the numbers tell us. The numbers, and the formula, provide verification. The formula, just like our definition of financial independence, is unbiased and verifiable.

Let's ignore inflation and taxes for now and see some examples. Say I earn $10,000 this month after taxes and my only source for that income is my job. This means my time-based income (TBI) is $10,000. Let's say my equity at the beginning of the month is $200,000. If my equity at the end of the month is also $200,000, then my change in equity or ΔE is a big fat zero. What does this mean? It means that I sacrificed my time to earn $10K and I consumed all $10K without increasing my equity. I have no equity growth. I did not pay off debt or save any money or earn a return on investments. My equity just stayed the same. I am a hamster on the financial wheel of life going nowhere. The FI metric should reflect that. We should expect the FI metric to show that I made no progress. We should expect FI=0. Now, we plug the numbers into our formula and get:

$$\Delta E = \$0$$
$$TBI = \$10,000$$

$$FI = \Delta E \: / \: TBI$$

$$FI = \$0/\$10,000 = 0$$

Perfect. The FI metric came out to zero just as expected. No equity growth equates to no financial freedom. My FI is zero. The world is a sad place for me at this point. You could say I have no financial independence. Or you could say that I am 100% financially dependent. You could even say that I am 100% wage slave. This matches the facts because what happened was that I worked all month to earn my $10K and I ended up right back where I started. I made no financial progress whatsoever. My paycheck is mandatory to maintain my lifestyle. So, next month I get to do the same thing all over again. This is living paycheck to paycheck. I am completely dependent on that paycheck for all of my financial needs. I have no financial freedom and no margin for error. Yuck! This is almost as bad as it gets. The only thing worse is to have a decline in equity.

Let's change the example to a better situation. Let's say I earn the same $10K and I start the month with the same $200K in equity. But, this time I end the month with equity of $204K. So, my change in equity or ΔE for this month is:

$$\Delta E = \$204,000 - \$200,000 = \$4,000.$$

This time, my FI metric numbers look like this.

$$\Delta E = \$4,000$$
$$TBI = \$10,000$$

$$FI = \Delta E \,/\, TBI$$

$$FI = \$4,000/\$10,000 = 40\%$$

This means that my FI is 40. Not bad. A heck of a lot better than the hamster on the wheel. I made significant forward progress. I am 40% financially independent. On the flip side, I am still 60% wage slave. I am somewhat dependent on my paycheck, but not totally. I am not independent enough to drop my time-based income, but I have some leeway. If I lost my job and took a pay cut of 10% or 20% it would be painful, but I would easily be able to absorb it. I am on my way to becoming financially independent.

Finally, consider the best situation of all. This time, I earn the same $10K and I start the month with the same $200K in equity. But, now I end the month with equity of $212K. So, my change in equity or ΔE for this month is $12,000. This time, my numbers look like this:

$$\Delta E = \$12,000$$
$$TBI = \$10,000$$

$$FI = \Delta E \,/\, TBI$$

$$FI = \$12,000 \,/\, \$10,000 = 120\%$$

This means that my FI is 120. Yippee-kai-yay baby, Life is good. You would say that I am 120% financially independent. Or you could say that I am 0% dependent on my job or 0% wage slave. Again, this matches the facts of what happened. I earned $10K, but my equity went up by $12K. So, either I paid off debt, or my investments earned money, or I saved money which increased my assets, or I have other non-time-based income. One way or another, my equity growth more than kept up with my time based income.

Why would we call this financially independent? Because I could have done away with my time-based income of $10K and instead just used $10K of my equity growth in its place if I had chosen to. I could have substituted some of my equity growth for my paycheck in order to maintain my lifestyle. I could have maintained my lifestyle without relying on time-based income. What it means is that I am not dependent on sacrificing my time to earn the $10K income. I could have maintained my lifestyle just fine without it.

As another example, I put together a little spreadsheet to show this process for a few months. In order to compute your FI, you need to have two balance sheets and you need to know your time-based income. Let's say Jack and Diane have determined that their TBI is $10,000 per month. And, let's assume they have typical assets and liabilities and that they are making some progress on growing their equity. They are slowly paying off some debts while also saving for retirement. The numbers are just made up but it will give you an idea of the overall process. The example shows four months' worth of following the plan. This gives them three months to compute their equity growth and FI. Jack and Diane have their FI floating around 24%. The full picture is as follows:

Jack and Diane - Balance Sheet and Statement of Financial Independence				
ASSETS	Jan-11	Feb-11	Mar-11	Apr-11
Primary Residence	$330,000.00	$331,000.00	$331,000.00	$331,000.00
Rental Property on E Street	$175,000.00	$175,000.00	$175,250.00	$175,500.00
Jacks 401K	$115,000.00	$115,700.00	$116,250.00	$117,000.00
Diane's 401K	$46,250.00	$45,750.00	$46,100.00	$46,150.00
Scottrade Investment Account	$32,800.00	$33,250.00	$33,350.00	$33,300.00
Chase Savings Account	$13,000.00	$13,250.00	$13,400.00	$13,400.00
Chase Checking Account	$4,350.00	$4,050.00	$4,150.00	$4,100.00
2009 Honda Accord	$12,850.00	$12,600.00	$12,400.00	$12,300.00
TOTAL ASSETS	$729,250.00	$730,600.00	$731,900.00	$732,750.00
LIABILITES				
Primary Mortgage	$240,000.00	$239,500.00	$238,990.00	$238,475.00
Rental Mortgage	$124,250.00	$123,750.00	$123,245.00	$122,737.00
Home equity line	$17,000.00	$16,800.00	$16,597.00	$16,393.00
MasterCard	$3,250.00	$3,500.00	$3,600.00	$3,800.00
Visa	$4,800.00	$5,200.00	$5,250.00	$5,225.00
Jacks Student Loan	$16,800.00	$16,650.00	$16,495.00	$16,300.00
Auto Loan on Accord	$14,500.00	$14,200.00	$13,895.00	$13,580.00
TOTAL LIABILITES	$420,600.00	$419,600.00	$418,072.00	$416,510.00
EQUITY	$308,650.00	$311,000.00	$313,828.00	$316,240.00
CHANGE IN EQUITY		$2,350.00	$2,828.00	$2,412.00
TIME BASED INCOME	$10,000.00	$10,000.00	$10,000.00	$10,000.00
FI		23.50%	28.28%	24.12%

Now that's a clear snapshot of where you stand financially. Look at all the questions that are answered from this:

- What are all of your assets?
- What are your assets' current values?
- What direction are your assets going in?
- Which assets are good assets?
- Which assets are bad assets?
- Are your total assets increasing or decreasing?
- What are all of your liabilities?
- What are your liabilities' current values?
- Are you paying down your liabilities?
- Do you have some liabilities that are creeping up?
- What is your equity (net worth)?
- Is your equity growing?
- How fast is your equity growing?
- Finally—and most importantly—what is your FI?

That's a lot of great information. And it takes very little time to gather it up. It shows your current position and trends. Most importantly, you can see what your financial independence level is as measured by FI. While all of the other information is important and useful, FI is what you should focus on. It's the utmost important metric when you are dealing with personal finances. Jack and Diane should be working on increasing that equity growth each month. They should do whatever it takes to get it up to and over their time-based income.

What makes this metric unique is that it combines the two primary financial statements together. It takes information from the balance sheet and the income statement and it combines it in a way that emphasizes the growth of equity on the balance sheet. Equity growth is what you are after. If you can grow your equity on a regular basis, then eventually you will be able to live off of that growth.

Few financial plans emphasize this relationship enough. The relationship between the income statement and the balance sheet is an important one. To understand it best, you should understand the nature of the two statements themselves.

> *If you can grow your equity on a regular basis, then eventually you will be able to live off of that growth.*

The income statement covers a period of elapsed time. You can create an income statement for a month, quarter, half year or full year. In contrast, the balance sheet is like a snapshot. It freezes everything in a moment in time. It is "as of" a particular date. The relationship we are interested in is how the income flows from the income statement onto the balance sheet. If you can efficiently transfer as much of your income as possible from the income statement to the balance sheet, then your equity growth will rise. This means that your FI will rise. Income either gets consumed, or it makes its way onto your balance sheet. It's one or the other. If you go on vacation, then that income is a pure expense and it will not be retained on your balance sheet. No equity growth. If you save it in an investment account or use it to pay down debt, then it gets retained on the balance sheet in an efficient manner. You get equity growth. The vacation leads to dependence. The investment leads to independence.

When you forgo consumption in order to transfer your income to your balance sheet, you have a choice to make. You can choose to pay off debt or you can choose to save or invest. You either reduce a debt or you increase an asset. Either way you grow your equity and that is the main thing we are after. Equity growth increases your financial independence and your FI will reflect that increase.

Now, let's get back to those two pesky items of inflation and taxes. First off, inflation. Most folks don't think much about inflation. But, inflation is insidious. It is the enemy of your equity because it makes it worth less and less every year. For those folks that are trying to live on a fixed income, inflation can be brutal. In order to combat this, your equity growth has to account for inflation. The growth in your equity must be enough to sustain your lifestyle *and* to keep up with inflation. Your goal isn't to be financially independent for a day or a year, it is to be financially independent FOREVER!

The formula I have given you so far doesn't account for inflation. To account for it, we are going to add an extra term to the formula. I call it the deflator. To come up with the proper deflator, you need to estimate two things. First, an expected rate of return for your equity investments. For example, if your equity is invested 100% in an S&P 500 index fund, then you could use an expected S&P 500 market rate. Second, we need the expected rate of inflation. As before, let's come up with some symbols for these components:

$$R = \text{Market Rate}$$
$$I = \text{Inflation Rate}$$

The formula for the deflator is just:

$$\text{Deflator} = (R-I) / R$$

If we use 10% as our market rate and 3% as our inflation rate, then we get:

$$R = 10\%$$
$$I = 3\%$$
$$\text{Deflator} = (.10-.03) / .10 = .7$$

So our deflator is 70% or .70.

To use the deflator with FI, we just multiply the simplified FI by the deflator. So, the complete formula is:

$$FI = \frac{\Delta E}{TBI} \times \frac{R - I}{R}$$

That formula measures financial independence *and* adjusts for inflation. In other words, it measures **perpetual financial independence**. Very cool!

Might I suggest to you to just go ahead and use .70 for the deflator while you are working on your FI. If you have reason to use a particular market rate or inflation rate, then go for it. But I think the .70 deflator is fine for most folks. The long-term rate of return of the S&P 500 is around 10% and the long-term rate of inflation is around 3%, so the .70 deflator is founded on good long-term data. If you want to be more conservative, then go ahead and use .65 or .60 if you want to.

If you don't trust me that the FI metric is accurate for measuring perpetual freedom, let me convince you with some hard numbers. As long as the estimates for R and I are accurate, then the FI metric formula really does represent perpetual financial independence. I'm going to use the suggested rates of R=.10 and I=.03 for this example. If your current TBI is $70,000 per year, then your equity growth needs to be:

Required Equity Growth = $70,000 / .07 = $100,000

This would require a total equity balance of $1M. If we call this year 1, then the FI calculation for year 1 is:

$\Delta E = 100,000$ $TBI = 70,000$ Deflator = .70
$FI = \Delta E / TBI \times .70$
$FI = 100,000 / 70,000 \times .70 = 1$

So, FI=100% for year 1. Since my claim is that the formula shows perpetual financial independence, we should be able to go out as many years as we like and still have an FI of 100%. In year 2, we don't want to have to live on $70,000. Inflation is present so we need to adjust. To stay at our current lifestyle, we need $70,000 x 1.03=$72,100 in year 2. In year 1 we had equity of $1M. Our equity growth was $100,000. $70,000 of that was consumed by us to support our lifestyle. The other $30,000 was added to equity. So in year 2 our equity is $1,030,000. How much equity growth does that produce for year 2? Just multiply by the market rate to find out.

Equity Growth = $1,030,000 x .10 = $103,000.

If we plug in the numbers for year 2 we get:

ΔE = 103,000   TBI = 72,100   Deflator = .70
FI = ΔE / TBI x .70
FI = 103,000 / 72,100 x .70 = 1

Perfection!. And so it will go if we compute these numbers out into infinity. Pick a year, any year, and your FI will be 100% forever more. Here is a table of twenty years:

Year	TBI	Equity Growth	Total Equity	Computed FI
1	$70,000	$100,000	$1,000,000	1
2	$72,100	$103,000	$1,030,000	1
3	$74,263	$106,090	$1,060,900	1
4	$76,491	$109,273	$1,092,727	1
5	$78,786	$112,551	$1,125,509	1
6	$81,149	$115,927	$1,159,274	1
7	$83,584	$119,405	$1,194,052	1
8	$86,091	$122,987	$1,229,874	1
9	$88,674	$126,677	$1,266,770	1
10	$91,334	$130,477	$1,304,773	1
11	$94,074	$134,392	$1,343,916	1
12	$96,896	$138,423	$1,384,234	1
13	$99,803	$142,576	$1,425,761	1
14	$102,797	$146,853	$1,468,534	1
15	$105,881	$151,259	$1,512,590	1
16	$109,058	$155,797	$1,557,967	1
17	$112,329	$160,471	$1,604,706	1
18	$115,699	$165,285	$1,652,848	1
19	$119,170	$170,243	$1,702,433	1
20	$122,745	$175,351	$1,753,506	1

You can see that by year 20, inflation has pushed up your cost of living to $122,745. But the system keeps growing your equity at the perfect rate to meet that need. Everything is in perfect balance. You are free–FOREVER!

Now, just one more thing to deal with–taxes. Remember that what we are doing here is replacing your time-based income with equity growth. If those two things are taxed at different rates, then we need to adjust for that. For example, if most of my equity is in a Roth IRA, then I really have a great advantage. Because when I go to pull money out of my equity growth engine, it will come out tax free. In contrast, if my equity is mostly in a traditional IRA, then I will have to pay tax on the money as I pull it out. Clearly, $2 million in a Roth is not the same as $2 million in a traditional IRA. I'm far better off with the Roth. The FI metric formula needs to account for this.

Even the traditional IRA will have a tax differential with TBI. When you invest in a traditional IRA, you still pay payroll taxes when the money goes in. But when the money comes out, no payroll taxes are charged. Beyond that, you may expect to have a different tax rate while you are earning versus the tax rate you will have when you start pulling money out of your equity growth. Tax rates may change, or you may move to a more tax-friendly state or you may be in a different tax bracket.

So, how do we handle all of this tax mess in the formula? We will treat everything on an after tax basis. We are already tracking TBI after taxes. Now we need to include the tax rate for our equity withdrawals. The only question is what rate to use. The bottom line is you are going to have to make some guesses about your tax rates. Your equity is probably a mixture of things. Some Roth, some traditional, some rental income, some capital gains and so on. Here again, just make your best guess as to what your tax rate will be on the equity that you use to replace your TBI. Let's call this your equity tax rate or ETR.. If you expect to pay no tax on your equity income, your ETR is zero. You have no adjustment to make. If you expect to pay some kind of tax, then just approximate your ETR and plug into the formula below. So, here is the final version of the FI formula:

$$FI = \frac{\Delta E}{TBI} \times \frac{R - I}{R} \times (1 - ETR)$$

And that, my friends, is personal financial planning perfection. This is a metric for financial independence, adjusted for inflation, and for tax differentials. Look no further—you have found the magic formula for personal financial success.

It might look a little messy to you, but the concepts are really simple. It's just equity growth divided by time-based income, adjusted by inflation and taxes. It's not like you are going to sit there with your calculator and figure this out every month. You are going to use software to do the work for you. You can use our free online system at *http://www.fimetric.com*. I know you can't see the numbers on this screen shot but you can see the general layout of the FI metric home page that you can use to follow the plan. It looks like this:

Conventional financial planning has nothing to compare to this. A typical financial plan will make some wild guess about how much money you should have in retirement and then it will work backwards from there to figure out how much money you should save each month or each year. Once the plan is done, it is stagnant. Set in stone. If something changes, you will need to throw that plan out and get a new one. The FI metric system is dynamic. It works on your numbers today. It uses your current lifestyle to determine what your needs are. It uses your current investments and financial decisions to figure out how you are doing. If something changes, the metric adapts. The FI metric system starts in the here and now and then projects forward. It automatically adjusts based on your financial results after every single month. It is specific, measurable, precise, dynamic and agile. It's far superior to the old way.

So what would our three financial stereotypes have to say about the FI metric? As expected, most pawns won't pay any attention. They just aren't thinking enough about their future to care. But, I think after they see all of the precision and logic that go into this, I might get lucky and turn a few pawns into gladiators.

For drones, this may be a turning point. Some are convinced and some are not. Those that remain drones will just stick with what they've got. What they have now makes them comfortable. They don't really want to see their FI. They probably would not like the result. It's like having a lump on your body. You know something is wrong but you don't go to the doctor because you are afraid. Maybe it's cancer. Maybe it's deadly. But you'd be better off to face your FI for what it is. It's the truth. It's a fact. Just like the cancer patient, you need treatment. Some drones bury their heads in the sand. Some will become Lance Armstrong style gladiators and go in for treatment.

And the gladiators are totally pumped up. Finally, they have something to focus on. The gladiator has always known that he is dependent on TBI and he hates it. Now he has a measurement that confirms his standing. Now he knows exactly where he is on the freedom scale. The gladiator will relentlessly pursue increases to his FI. As with equity growth, he will measure it every month. He can't wait to measure it and see if he has improved. He dreams of the day that his FI will finally hit 100% and he does whatever he can to draw that day closer and closer.

Long Live the Gladiator !

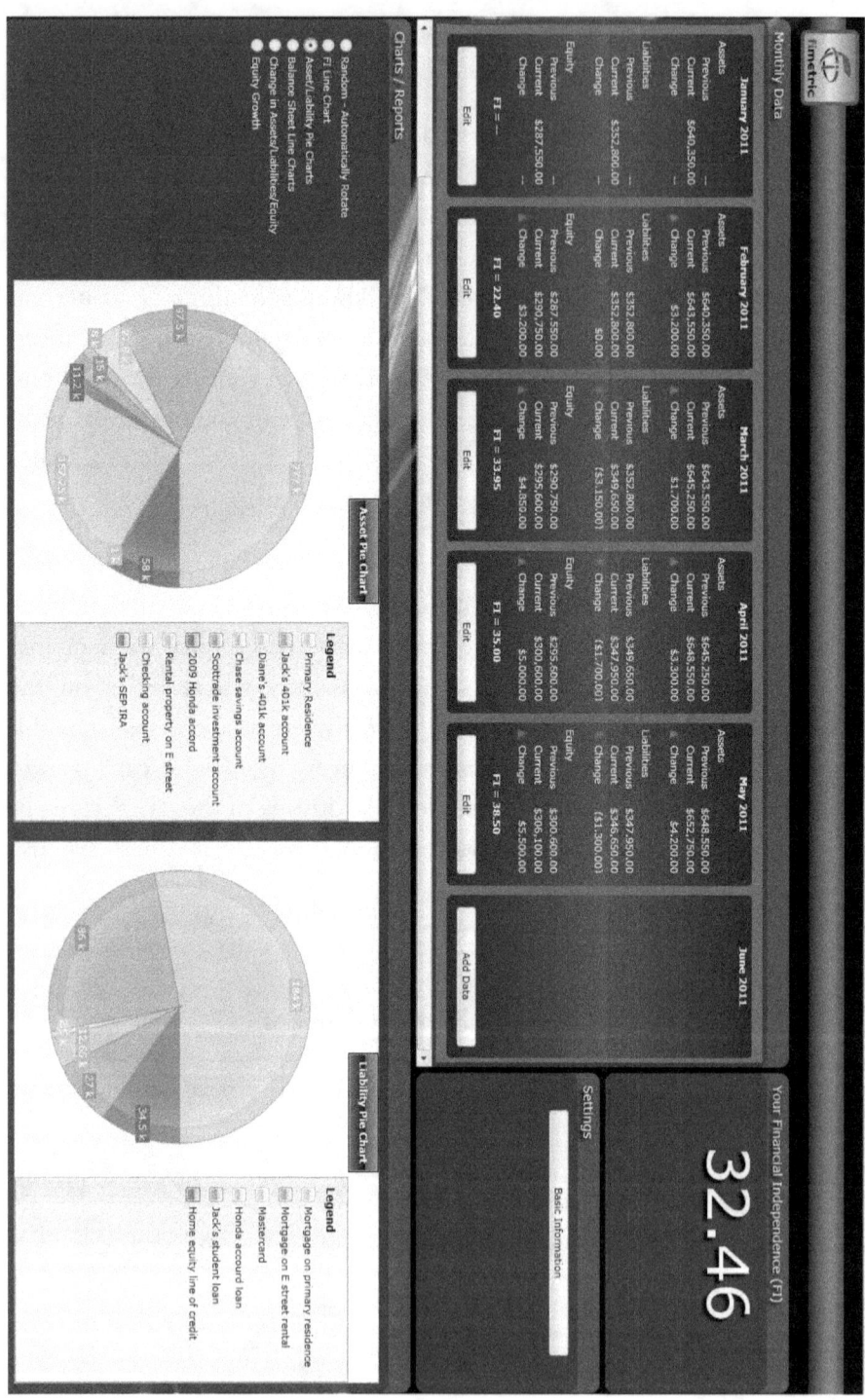

CHAPTER 4 KEYNOTES

1. Don't trust your financial future to a plan with no metric

2. Financial Independence can be measured with a simple formula

3. Measure your FI every month

CHAPTER 5
TIME VALUE OF MONEY

"We must use time as a tool, not as a crutch."

~ John Fitzgerald Kennedy

In the field of finance, there are a number of formulas that are used to compute the value of investments over time. They are referred to as time value of money (TVM) calculations. The most common of these is a simple formula called future value. I want to familiarize you with this formula in order to help expose flaws in conventional financial planning. The future value formula allows you to compute what an investment made today will be worth sometime in the future assuming a certain rate of return. There are three parts to the future value formula: Amount (A), Rate (R), and Time (T). Since our goal is to reduce our dependence on time-based income, it is very important for us to understand how our investments grow over time. That's what the future value of money formula tells you. And those three parts of the formula are all important. The formula itself is pretty simple.

$$FV = A(1+R)^T$$

The simplest example is to look at an investment for just one year.

Say we invest $1,000 for a year at 8%. Plugging into the formula we get:

$$FV = \$1,000 \times (1.08)^1 = \$1,080$$

This tells us that if we invest $1,000 and we earn a rate of return of 8%, then we will end up with $1,080 after one year. Not very interesting for just one year. But this formula is how financial folks are able to give examples saying that if you invest $10,000 today and earn 8% for 40 years you will end up with $217,245. Just plug in the numbers.

$$FV = \$10,000 \times (1.08)^{40} = \$217,245$$

Yeah–now that's more interesting. It's handy to know how to determine the future value of money. Now you can do it on your own. But the real reason I am introducing the time value of money formula to you is that I want to discuss the three parts of the equation. Amount, Rate and Time.

$$FV = A(1+R)^T$$

While all three components are important, it is (T) or Time that I want to focus on. Let's talk about Amount and Rate first and then we will get into the Time part in great detail.

Let's start with (A) or Amount. You've heard the saying that it takes money to make money. Well, it's definitely true in the investing world. (A) is simply the amount that you have available to invest. Of course, the more you have, the better. Generally speaking, you will start off with a small amount and it will grow over time. So, to get a large (A) in the formula, we generally have to work at it for many years. Unless your rich uncle dies or you win the lottery, you will just have to keep adding amounts to your (A) and let your investment growth also increase the (A) with returns year after year. From a personal finance point of view, you will want to save as much as you can on expenses and cost of living so that you can make your invested amount as high as possible. The more you can pour in, the more it will grow. That's what the future value of money formula tells us. The bottom line is that you should do whatever you can to maximize (A). Save, conserve, and invest.

You have a lot of control over the amount of your investment. Your behaviors and habits regarding your financial choices can dramatically change the amount available for investment. As consumers, we make these financial decisions on a daily basis. Spend today to enjoy something in the short term and you have forgone the opportunity of using that money to increase (A) and get your future value cranking higher and higher. As you make financial choices, pause and consider that your decision to spend now will lead to this lost opportunity. Once it's spent, you can't get it back. Make good choices and do everything you can to maximize the amount available for investment. Change your perspective and replace status symbols like fancy cars, clothes and vacations with a better symbol of financial success, a bigger pool of money to invest with. Do what you can to maximize (A) and your future value will increase.

Now let's move on to the rate of return (R). Your rate of return will depend on what you have your (A) invested in. You have many choices here. In the personal finance world, typical investments include real estate, stocks, bonds, money markets and gold. There are plenty of other things to chose from, but those are the most common. (R) is the part of the formula that we would like to somehow magically make large. It would be sensational if we could earn a great rate of return. That would be the easiest way to reach our goal. We would not need a lot of money and we would not need a lot of time. Unfortunately, academic research and real life experience tells us that our investment markets are very efficient. That means it is generally hard to beat the market rate of return. There are lots of books on the subject of trying to outpace market returns. Jim Cramer, famous hedge fund investor and host of Mad Money, is a great example of someone who is always trying to beat the market. Jim's got a great informative and entertaining

TV show. He always tries to look out for the little guy. If it's your passion to become a great stock investor, then you should read some of Jim's books and watch his show. Jim does a great job of presenting stock investing in terms that work for personal finance. But, it's extremely hard to beat the market and often when people try, they end up underperforming. So, take it slow. If you are new to stock investing, then start off with simpler things like index funds. Then, you can gradually start trading individual stocks. (BOOYAH! Cramer)

You also have control over the rate of return you get by deciding what markets or asset classes to invest in. Investing in your own business has the potential to provide the greatest return. It also involves the most risk. The stock market is next in line. The returns are good and the risk is less than what you have when you start your own business. In contrast, money markets provide the lowest returns. The trade-off for a higher return is greater risk. Higher risk demands a higher return. Depending on your age and circumstances, you should balance your investment portfolio in a well diversified collection of assets of an appropriate risk level. What to invest in is a balancing act. You can't be too conservative or you will never build enough of an investment pool to generate sufficient income to fund your lifestyle. You have to take risk. In summary, (R) is something that we would love to make large. It would make life really easy for us. But we generally accept what the market gives us and invest in assets appropriate for our risk level.

Finally, let's talk about (T) or Time. (T) is the most powerful component in the formula. We have all heard the term "exponential growth" or "exponential rate." Those terms are used to describe things that grow very fast. A virus, for example, has the potential to spread exponentially. If you are the first person to catch a virus then the total count of infected people is 1. Then you infect 5 people, so the total count is 6. Then each of those 5 people infect 5 more so the total count is 31. And so on. With just a few cycles, the numbers grow dramatically. Exponential growth is most impressive when the exponent gets large. The growth in cycle one of our example was 5. The growth in cycle 2 was 25. If we kept going, we would see that the growth in cycle 10 is 5^{10}=9.7 million. Pretty amazing after only 10 cycles. And it would just get more amazing after that. At an ever-increasing rate of growth.

The same thing happens with future value of money. The growth rate due to compounding is exponential. And, the most dramatic growth will occur when the time period is very long. Time is the exponential factor in the future value formula and it is the most powerful part of the equation.

Since time is the powerhouse part of the equation, we should do whatever we can to maximize its value. But how do we make the most of time in the formula? The answer is that we have to focus on the (A) amount in the formula. We want to make the (A) as large as possible and we want to do it as early as possible. For us, the (A) is our equity. We want to increase our equity as much as possible and we want to do it as soon as possible so that time can work its exponential magic for us. Exponential equity growth. That's what we are after.

I have heard the term *debt snowball* used a lot in personal finance. I like the term snowball because it gives good imagery for exponential growth. The little snowball starts rolling down the hill and grows slowly. As it grows, it has the ability to pick up more and more snow and its growth rate accelerates dramatically. However, I don't really care so much about the debt snowball. I'd rather focus on the equity snowball. Whether I am growing my equity through savings or through the payment of debt or through appreciation in asset values doesn't make all that much difference to me. I just want to grow that equity as much as possible. If paying off debt is the best way, great. If investing makes my equity grow faster, even better. It just depends on the options that I have available. As my equity snowball grows, it picks up more equity along the way. It gets bigger and then it picks up even more equity. It's exponential growth in action.

The Rate and Time parts of the future value formula combine to form what is called the future value factor. You can create a table of future value factors and then apply them to any amount to get the value of a current amount at some time in the future. Here is a small table of future value factors:

Future Value Factors					
	5%	8%	10%	12%	15%
5 Years	1.28	1.47	1.61	1.76	2.01
10 Years	1.63	2.16	2.59	3.11	4.05
15 Years	2.08	3.17	4.18	5.47	8.14
20 Years	2.65	4.66	6.73	9.65	16.37
25 Years	3.39	6.85	10.83	17.00	32.92
30 Years	4.32	10.06	17.45	29.96	66.21
35 Years	5.52	14.79	28.10	52.80	133.18
40 Years	7.04	21.72	45.26	93.05	267.86
45 Years	8.99	31.92	72.89	163.99	538.77
50 Years	11.47	46.90	117.39	289.00	1083.66

To read this, you take the interest rate at the top and the number of years along the left and then find the intersection of the two to get the future value factor. For example, an investment made at 10% for 20 years will be worth 6.73 times as much as the original investment amount. Likewise, an investment made at 12% for 40 years will be worth 93 times as much as the original amount. Look at the amazing result for 15% and 50 years. You would have more than 1,000 times the original amount if you could pull that off.

Notice how the future value factors grow dramatically faster as the time values get larger. The following graph shows the exponential growth rates of these five rates of return.

Future Value Factor Graphs

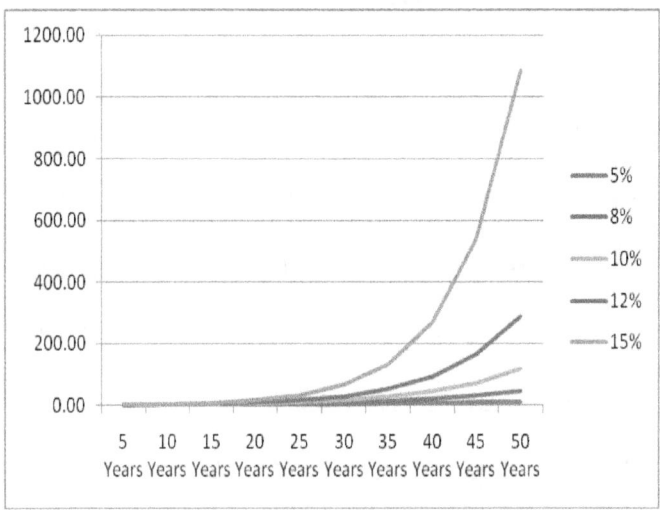

You can see how those lines start shooting skyward steeper and steeper as each year passes. The more years you have to let your returns compound, the more TVM will work for you. If you can let time work long enough, then it will take the heavy lifting out of your financial journey.

The future value factor graph illustrates how fast the growth due to compounding increases over time. Consider the next graph which shows the growth of a $10,000 investment at 8% for 50 years. After 50 years of growth, your $10,000 investment will have grown to over $469,000. But the important thing about the graph is that it shows the growth as three different components. First, the original investment is shown, then the growth due to simple interest, and finally the growth due to compound interest. If you are viewing this chart in black and white, you really need to get the color version. It shows massive compounding in the later years. You can see the color version on the FImetric website at www.fimetric.com.

$10,000 Invested at 8% for 50 Years

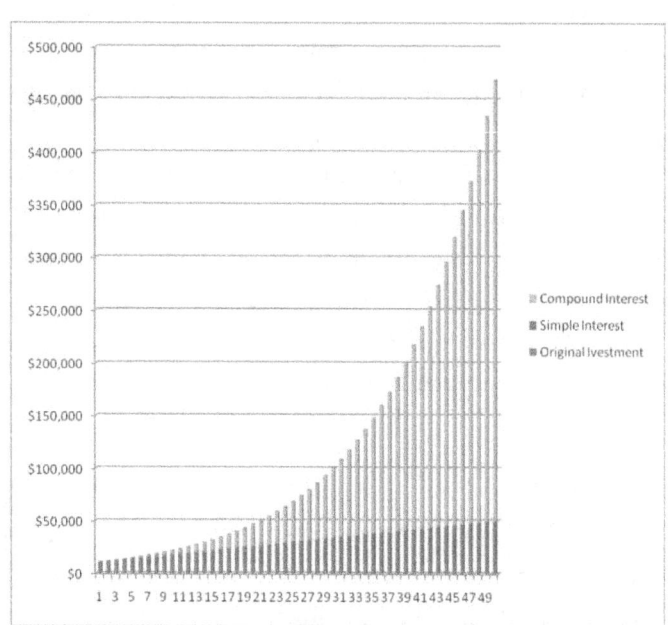

I can't think of a clearer picture than that for illustrating the amazing potential of compound growth. It's the interest on the interest that can take the heavy lifting out of your financial efforts. As you can see, it dwarfs all other factors. By the time this investment reaches years 30 and higher, the compound interest dominates the landscape.

But, as you can see, it takes a while for that growth to kick in. In the first years of a compound interest graph, the compounding component is miniscule. It's only significant if it has enough investment periods to shift into hyper growth mode. It's the out years where that hyper growth takes place. And the only way to get there is to start as soon as possible. To start early and let time work. If you start late, then you miss out on the hyper growth as shown on the graph. If you start late, you are going to have to do the heavy lifting on your own. Compounding is not going to help much.

As I've been saying all along, a financial gladiator doesn't want to wait 40 or 50 years to become financially independent. A financial gladiator is fighting for his freedom right now–this month. A 40 or 50 year horizon is not part of the plan. That said, what is a gladiator to do to maximize compound interest? You do exactly what you would do without it. You work as hard as you can right now to increase your equity and increase your FI. You are doing this in order to get your freedom as soon as possible not in order to capitalize on compound interest. But, it turns out, that the gladiator approach is exactly the best approach that there is in order to maximize the effects of compounding. That's because the gladiator has a sense of urgency in his plan.

Hopefully, this detour into the math behind TVM has helped to show the power of compounding in investment returns. And, hopefully it helps show the importance of time. TVM can really give you a solid understanding of long-term personal financial planning.

To summarize our look at time value of money, we can see that there are three essential components in investing: Amount (A), Rate (R) and Time (T). We want to maximize all three. But, most important of all, we want to put time on our side. Time is the exponential component in the time value of money formula and it has incredible power to turn modest investments into large sums over long periods.

CHAPTER 5 KEYNOTES

1. Investment returns are determined by three components Amount, Rate and Time

2. Time is the exponential growth factor

3. Start now

CHAPTER 6
FI = 100 ASAP

"I think there is some connection between absolute discipline and absolute freedom."

~ Alan Rickman

There is some blatant hypocrisy in the personal finance community when it comes to certain advice. Especially advice that has time at its core. If there are any pawns or drones left out there, pay attention to this chapter. It is especially designed for you.

Just about any financial book you pick up will have something similar to the previous chapter. Somewhere along the way, the author will extol the virtues of compound interest. I extol those virtues too. It's just that I don't plan on waiting around for those powerful exponential returns to start kicking in. I want to get something done sooner. But the hypocrites don't take that approach. On the one hand, the tell you about compound interest and then on the other hand, they give you some slow road financial plan to follow. What the heck? Do they believe in compound interest or not? If they believe in it, then they ought to be telling you to save as much as you can as early as you can. To suggest anything else is hypocritical.

Consider the lousy advice of using a fixed savings rate. I often hear or read the advice that you should be trying to save 15% of your income for retirement. Sometimes they use 10%, sometimes they use 20%. I have even seen charts that tell you what percentage of income to save at a particular age. They say, for example, if you are under 30, then you should be saving 10% of your income, while if you are over 40, then the magic rate should be 15%. Where in the world do these magic numbers come from? There is absolutely no basis in finance for such numbers. We just spent an entire chapter talking about how important time was and how it is the most powerful tool in equity growth. So why in the world would an advisor tell you to save a fixed percentage of your income? An advisor who tells you to save 15% when it is within your means to save 16% is doing you financial harm. Fire him. You can do better on your own.

I know the reason why those advisors use those fixed rates. It's because they want to make their clients feel good. They want to make their clients feel like they have a good plan. But it's all marketing and salesmanship. It has nothing to do with good financial advice. A good advisor should grow a spine and tell you that you need to save as much as you possibly can. If you can save 80% then by all means do it. You'll be financially independent in no time if you can put away that much.

In order to get hyper growth from compound interest, you should save as much as you possibly can and you should do it as early as possible. This is the most important thing that you can learn about investing for personal finance. Let me repeat:

In order to get hyper growth from compound interest, you should save as much as you possibly can and you should do it as early as possible.

There is no fixed percentage. Not when you are 25, not when you are 35, not when you are 40, not at any age. Time value of money tells us clearly that you should save as much as you can as soon as you can - period. So, having a fixed percentage as a target is just plain bad advice. You should be trying to squeeze out every extra dollar that you can and you should do it as soon as possible. Look at the compound interest graph from the last chapter one more time.

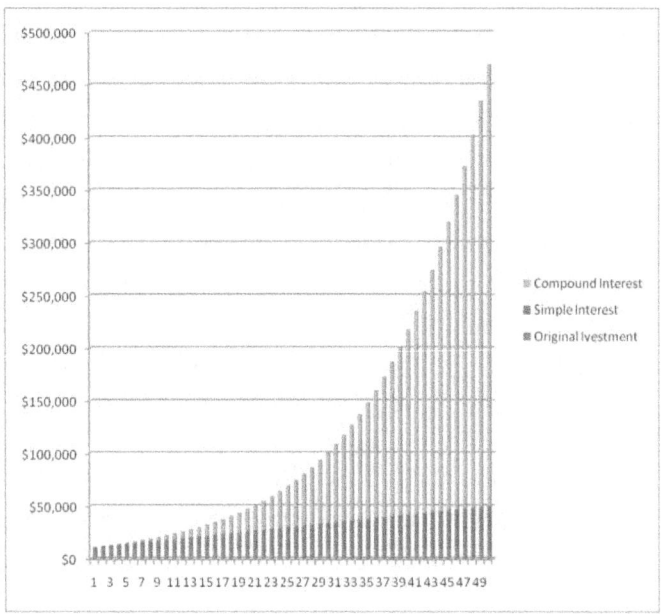

If you delay, if you stall, if you take your time about the process, then you will not enjoy those spectacular compounded returns that are displayed on the right side of the graph. Any advice that calmly tells you to do anything other than save as much as possible as soon as possible will take away some of that spectacular growth. Do not listen to the rules of thumb for saving 15% of your income or 20% of your income. That advice is garbage. Understand the power of compound growth and the fact that it is the later years where most of the growth happens. Then you should clearly understand the importance of putting urgency into your financial plan. Do not delay. Start now and invest as much as possible as soon as possible.

There is yet another bogus technique I have seen used that I refer to as "threading the needle." A client comes in to an advisor and the advisor spends a few hours with him or her finding out about the client's financial situation. Then, the advisor uses all of his skill and training to craft a plan so that the client can meet his or her retirement goals at just the right time. The client wants to retire at age 62 and wants to have a certain annual income at that age. So the advisor crunches a bunch of numbers using time value of money software to precisely determine how much the client needs to save in order to accomplish the goal at just the right time. The advisor determines that the client is in good shape and that he or she only needs to save 12.4% of current income to meet the goal. This makes the client feel good. The client is impressed with the advisor's mastery of the numbers. The advisor then prints out the plan with some nice pretty charts and numbers to back them up. The client pays a fee and everyone is happy. They have successfully threaded the needle.

The only problem is that this entire process is just a big charade. You are going to bet your financial future on a 40 year plan full of a bunch of estimates and assumptions. The planning of the Apollo 11 moon shot that put Neil Armstrong on the moon was a lot more reliable than your crazy 40 year "thread the needle" financial plan. It's the equivalent of financial planning snake oil. What a joke!

Threading the needle like this makes a mockery of what time value of money really tells us. You should take those pretty charts and numbers and put them right through your shredder because they are not just worthless, they are harmful. What time value of money tells us is that time is important. And the way we should interpret that is that we need a sense of urgency or immediacy in our financial plan. We should not put off until tomorrow what we can do today, because tomorrow it will be more difficult for us. Tomorrow, compounding has less time to do the heavy lifting for us. Time will be less helpful for us as it ticks by. If we try to precisely thread the financial needle, then we are just stretching out time to the last possible moment. Bad advice. Terrible advice. It takes one of the most powerful financial tools you have, and it reduces its potency.

Consumption smoothing is the latest variation of this snake oil to come onto the scene. Economists have jumped into the personal finance arena with this wonderful tool that they have created. Their idea is that some people are saving too little and others are actually saving too much. They believe that what is needed is a smoothing out of this process over a person's lifetime. They believe that you should determine your appropriate standard of living and then you should maintain that standard throughout your life. Smooth, and steady. To accomplish this, they claim to have figured out some sophisticated computer algorithms that can accurately determine exactly how much you should be consuming and saving at each stage of your life. They say they can determine your highest possible standard of living which can be maintained. The software takes in all kinds of inputs, demographics, tax factors, ages, family unit information and so on. Then it chugs and chugs and … bing, out comes the magic number. Their computer has determined what your standard of living should be for the rest of your life. Excuse me while I pick myself up off the floor. I was laughing so hard I fell out of my chair.

I hope that by now you can see that consumption smoothing is pure nonsense. It's being sold to you because these people make money off of their ideas and their software. Hey, I can't blame them. It's hard to make a living as an economist. Why not convert your ideas to something the masses will buy into?

Don't believe this nonsense. Do you really think that their software can tell YOU what YOUR standard of living should be? I will determine my own standard of living thank you very much. Further, my standard of living is not defined by how much I consume. The consumption smoothing proponents would have you believe that your life is defined by how much junk you buy. If you don't consume your maximum amount smoothly over your lifetime, then you are somehow being deprived. Nonsense. Don't define your life by what you consume. What a pathetic state to be in. Can't you work on your financial independence with intensity and urgency AND enjoy life? I think so. I don't think we need the consumption smoothers to tell us how to live.

Instead, do the best you can to increase your financial independence as much as possible and as soon as possible. And find ways to enjoy life along the way. If you ever run across one of these consumption smoothers, just laugh at him and show him the chart on compound interest. Have him buy your lunch and tell him that it's just part of his computed consumption level. Maybe you will cross paths with a consumption smoothing proponent sometime in the future. Maybe by then you will be financially independent and he will still be smoothing out his consumption. You might see him on the freeway on his way to work while you are heading out to the golf course. Hmmm, consumption smoothing—yeah right.

Please, please, please—don't buy into any of these stupid ideas. There is no target savings rate. There is no target consumption rate. There is no magic retirement number out there for you. All of these schemes are just hocus pocus nonsense. They throw you off the real path to success which is based on tracking your financial independence and improving it as much as possible and as soon as possible. The right track is to put in the hard efforts now, today, and make significant progress on your financial freedom.

Tell the snake oil vendors to take their fancy charts, algorithms and new economic terms and stick em where the sun don't shine. They are all sub optimal when it comes to personal finance and financial independence. Ignore anyone pimping anything that remotely looks like that kind of garbage. Keep it simple and focus on your financial independence. Just do as much as you can to increase your FI. And do it now. Do it this month and every month. End of story.

In chapter one, I said that your goal should be to attain financial independence. Now that we have covered TVM and compound interest, let me modify that goal. Your goal is FI=100 ASAP. Make it your prime directive. At the end of your yoga class, chant it out loud. Everyone is getting tattoos these days. When the tat artist asks you what you want, tell him you want FI=100 ASAP and you want it big. Change your license plate to FI 100. Name your first kid FI, your second kid hundred and your third kid ASAP. If you have a dog named Fido, drop the "do" part and call him FI. You get the point. Set FI=100 ASAP as your goal and make it important to you.

The goal should bring thoughts of focus, determination and urgency to your mind. You should make changes and decisions in your financial life that take effect NOW. And forget about the savings rate or any other goofy financial trickery that you have heard of. Those things will only complicate your financial life and produce no extra benefit. The only metric that matters is FI. It is comprehensive in nature and oh so much better than things like savings rates. What is the difference between saving $1,000 and paying off a debt of $1,000? If you are monitoring savings rate, then you get no credit for paying off debt. FI includes everything. It is the perfect metric to monitor your financial health.

The sense of immediacy that FI=100 ASAP should bring is a desire to increase your FI right now–this month, today. If your FI was 15 last month, try to make it 16 this month–or 15.5 or even 15.1. Just squeeze out every possible increase that you can. There is no increase that is so small as to be insignificant. Every little bit counts. Saving more and saving early is the only way to maximize the benefits of exponential growth. Getting your financial independence earlier in life will maximize your enjoyment of your freedom.

I have heard it said of personal finance that it is a marathon not a sprint. I won't deny that becoming financially independent may be a long process. So it's easy to fall into the notion that it is a marathon. But you should think the opposite way. If you want to maximize the benefits of time, then you need to realize that it is a sprint, not a marathon. If you think in marathon terms, then you will be taking out the urgency of the moment and you will lose the power of time. If you think in sprint terms, then you will do whatever you need to in the current moment in order to get closer to the finish line. I'm not saying that you will become financially independent in a short amount of time. What I am saying is that you should try to get there as quickly as possible because mathematics proves to us that time is a powerful financial tool and the right way to leverage time is to do as much as we can today. It could take years or maybe even decades to become financially independent, but you should continue to look at it as a sprint–not a marathon.

I have used the comparison between fitness and finances several times now. But there is one way in which they differ greatly. In fitness, it gets harder and harder to get better results the more fit you get. It's easier to lose the first 20 pounds than it will be to lose the next 20. In finances, it's just the opposite. It starts off hard and then it gets easier as time goes by. If you start off working as hard as you can on your equity snowball, then it will grow and start working for you. The bigger your equity snowball gets, the more work it does. Eventually, the work it does will dwarf the work that you are doing.

I hope you have not wasted your money on a glitzy 40 year financial plan from some financial advisor. If you have, fire up that shredder and get rid of it. You need to focus your energy today and make the necessary changes to increase your FI right now. That way the future will be easier because time will have longer to work in your favor. This concept of time and immediacy and urgency is important. It's easy to understand the power of time, and at the same time dismiss its importance. It happens all the time in the personal financial world. It even happens to renowned financial planners as they give advice.

There are a few universally accepted truths in the financial planning community. Probably the foremost accepted statement is "start early." The idea is that time is your best friend. It is a powerful component in taking the heavy lifting out of financial independence. But sometimes those renowned advisors give some conflicting advice. I listened once while a 67-year-old woman who had no savings asked a planner for help. He told her not to worry because it's never too late. Well, I got news for you. Sometimes it is too late. To say otherwise is to contradict the truth that time is your best friend. You can't have it both ways. If time is your best friend when you are young, then time is your worst enemy when you are getting on in years. I'm not saying that a financial planner should tell an unprepared elderly person to give up. But if they have waited too long, it's going to be a near impossible battle. All you can do is damage control. Make the best of the situation, but acknowledge the fact that you are too late to generate enough equity to maintain your lifestyle. Something is going to have to give. Don't let that happen to you. Remember your mantra. FI=100 ASAP.

A recent *Wall Street Journal* article confirms my view point. The article called "Retirement Boomers Find 401(k) Plans Fall Short" found that the 401(k) savings for retirement aged people where only 25% of what was needed to maintain their standard of living. How would you like to reach retirement age and find out you need to scale back your lifestyle by 75%? Ouch. I wonder what kind of plan these folks were following. Was it the 10% plan, the "thread the needle plan"? Or maybe they were consumption smoothers. Stupid advice with devastating results. It's too late for these folks to make up for it. Time is now their enemy, not their friend. They will likely work the rest of their lives just to stay afloat.

I guarantee you that we will never see a *Wall Street Journal* article titled "Retirement Boomers Regret Having Saved Too Much Money." It just isn't going to happen. If you are going to err, then which side do you want to err on? Saving too much or saving too little? The truth is that you are not going to over save. Trust in the numbers not in the rhetoric. If your FI is less than 100, you still have more saving to do.

Don't follow the slow road to financial independence. Don't believe the consumption smoothers who tell you that maybe you are over saving. Don't try to thread the needle. Save now. Get focused now. Increase your FI now. FI=100 ASAP–Period. Don't delay, don't procrastinate, don't take the slow route. Get focused, get energized and make changes today. That is the best way to get time on your side. Oh, one more thing:

FI=100 ASAP!

CHAPTER 6 KEYNOTES

1. Fixed savings rates are stupid

2. Save as much as you can as soon as you can

3. Make your goal FI=100 ASAP

CHAPTER 7
FI PROJECTION

"Inflation is as violent as a mugger, as frightening as an armed robber and as deadly as a hit man."

~Ronald Reagan

The FI metric plan just keeps getting better and better. Just when you thought you had enough incredible financial planning breakthroughs, I've got even more stuff for you. After I started using the FI metric plan myself, I got to thinking. Wouldn't it be nice if I could determine the date when I would finally reach FI=100? After fiddling around for a while, I finally got it. Just grab a magic eight ball. Ask the great eight ball oracle if you will be financially free within 5 years. Shake it up and read what it says. If you are following the FI metric plan, it will always say:

"It is certain".

If you are following some other dumb plan, then the eight ball will always say:

"Outlook not so good"

Although I consider the magic eight ball to be a higher authority than most financial gurus, I think we might want to have something to back it up. Mathematics will do the job. The math behind the FI metric is pretty simple. But if we crank it up a notch, then we can do something really amazing. We can project your FI into the future. This is the exact reverse of the current financial planning industry process. What most financial planners do is to pick some date in the future and some number to shoot for at that date. They base everything on that projection and then they move backward in time to today. They figure out some silly percentage or dollar amount to save and they program the drones to follow the plan. Then the drones follow the plan and find out that it was not quite what it should have been. And they find out when it's too late to do anything about it.

In contrast, the FI metric plan works on the here and now. We measure our financial independence today and we work diligently to increase it every single month until it hits 100. When it finally does hit 100, we can be relieved that we didn't follow any stupid backward plans. We can feel relief because we are free. That date when we hit FI=100 is our FI date. It's like the birth of a new being. The wage slave is dead. A free person is born. Your FI date will be a day of celebration for sure. I am sure you will be doing a back flip on that day. So, I really, really hope it happens before you turn 80. Because doing a back flip when you're 80 is dangerous. Hey, the sooner, the better. Get it done while you are as young as possible so that you can enjoy life to the fullest.

Pawns don't know what an FI date is. They have no plan. Drones do have a plan, but their FI date is fixed in time. Probably 40 or 50 years from now. Or maybe never, since the plan is not dynamic and adaptable. The drone follows his plan and waits for the day to arrive. A FI metric gladiator does not wait. A FI metric gladiator reaches into the future and pulls his FI date backward in time as much as possible. To the gladiator, the FI date is dynamic just like his plan is. If his plan is going well, the FI date moves closer. If his plan is going poorly, then the FI date moves away into the future. A gladiator works on things today so that his FI date will get here sooner rather than later. He adjusts and adapts and does whatever it takes to make that FI date as early as possible. Let's check out the math for determining your FI date.

The formulas in this chapter are somewhat complicated in terms of mathematics. You are definitely not going to compute this stuff on your own. You need software or at least a spreadsheet to do it. But the concept is still very simple. We are just going to use time value of money formulas to compute what your FI will be in the future. Of course we don't want to get too carried away with this. The formulas use estimates for expected rate of return and expected inflation rate. So these projections, although mathematically sound, are not to be taken too literally. That said, they are great as supporting information for motivation. They become more and more accurate as you near your FI date. They adapt as you compute them over time. When you follow the system you know where you stand. Keep computing your FI and your FI date every month.

What a motivator it will be to see the good decisions that you make pull your FI date closer and closer in time to where you are now. Don't be discouraged if your FI date is far into the future at the moment. It is what it is. If you are following the FI metric system, then you will find ways to draw it closer and closer over the years as you become more financially efficient. Whatever you do, don't ignore it. The facts are the facts. If you ignore them, then you will be flying with the drones again.

If the math in this section is more than you want to deal with, then just skim through it. I won't blame you at all. The formulas are messy. If you'd like to, you can skip the details and simply trust me that they are based on sound TVM formulas. All that I am doing is combining my FI metric formula with some more detailed TVM formulas. Skip the details and trust the results if you'd like to. I'm not making anything up, I am just using sound mathematics in a new way. For the brave at heart, here comes the math.

By now, you know the formula for FI. Here it is again for your enjoyment:

$$FI = \frac{\Delta E}{TBI} \times \frac{R - I}{R} \times (1 - ETR)$$

Now, I will establish the formula for FI(N), where N is some period into the future. For example, if you want to see what your FI will be in 5 years, you just compute FI(5). Just plug in whatever value you want to for N and you can see a projection of what your FI will be in the future.

To compute FI(N), we just need to know the components of the FI metric for year N. Plugging these into the FI formula we get.

$$FI(N) = \frac{\Delta E(N)}{TBI(N)} \times \frac{R - I}{R} \times (1 - ETR)$$

All we really need to do is to come up with $\Delta E(N)$ and TBI(N). The rest of the formula is the same as the standard FI formula. TBI(N) is pretty easy. It's just a forward adjusted version of your current time-based income. You have to estimate the rate at which your TBI will increase. We will call that rate of change TBIR. As an estimate for TBIR, you might want to use the same rate as you use for the inflation rate. Hopefully your wages are at least keeping up with inflation. If you are getting promotions and climbing the wage ladder, you may want to use something higher like 5%. Once you settle on a rate, we just use the future value of a lump sum formula to get your TBI in the future.

$$TBI(N) = TBI (1+TBIR)^N$$

$\Delta E(N)$ is harder. This is asking what will your equity growth be in year N. You should remember how important equity growth is. For someone trying to become financially independent, equity growth is the name of the game. The fact that we can come up with a formula to project what your equity growth will be sometime in the future is a pretty cool concept. To figure out what your *equity growth* will be, we need to know what your *equity* will be in the last two years of the projection. If we let E(N) be your equity in year N, then we want to get your equity in year N and in year N-1. Once we have that, then we just subtract E(N)-E(N-1) and we have $\Delta E(N)$.

$$\Delta E(N) = E(N) - E(N-1)$$

There are two parts to figuring out what your equity will be in the future: market returns and new investment. Every year when you work on your FI, you are adding new money to your equity. Also, the equity that you currently have is growing because of investment returns. These two combine to create your equity growth. We need a formula for E(N) which includes both of these parts.

Figuring out what your market returns will be on your current equity is just another simple future value of a lump sum calculation. We just take your current equity and project it into the future using the expected market rate. The harder part is to determine how much your equity will grow due to your contributions—your new investments. To figure this out, we need to know how much you are contributing now. Then to project it, we need to know what rate of change to use as you increase your contributions over time. We will call the investment amount C for capital and we will call the rate of change RC.

So if you are adding 30K per year to your equity as new capital, and you think you can increase that contribution by 3% per year, you would use C=10,000 and RC=.03. The proper formula to use here is the TVM formula for a growing annuity. The future value of this growing annuity is computed with this formula:

$$FV(N) = C \times \frac{(1+R)^N - (1+RC)^N}{(R-RC)}$$

Here, R is the market rate and RC is the rate of change for C which is the current new capital investment amount. That formula will tell you how much your equity will have grown due to your new capital contributions from today through year N.

Now we have to add in the equity growth that occurs due to market returns. Since you know what your equity is today, we just use the future value of a lump sum formula to get us the value of this part of your equity in the future. The future value of your equity with no additional contributions would be:

$$E(N) = E(1+R)^N$$

But, as we have said, you are also adding new contributions. So we need to combine both parts to get the full formula for E(N):

$$E(N) = C \times \frac{(1+R)^N - (1+RC)^N}{(R-RC)} + E(1+R)^N$$

That formula will give you the dollar value of your equity in year N. That value will be comprised of market returns and new investment. Pretty cool stuff. Plug your numbers into that formula and you can project what your equity amount will be sometime in the future. This is the opposite of conventional planning which starts with some goal in the future and then works backward. Here we are starting with present values and then working forward. Much more logical.

Well, I warned you these would get messy. Hold on to your shorts because it's going to get worse. For the FI metric, we don't really care about the equity value itself in year N. We want to know what the change in equity is going to be. We need $\Delta E(N)$. Since we know how to get $E(N)$, we can get the two numbers we need to get $\Delta E(N)$. All we need is your equity in the last two years of the projection. That is $E(N)$ and $E(N-1)$. Then we can get $\Delta E(N)$ by a simple subtraction as $E(N)-E(N-1)$.

$$\Delta E(N) = E(N) - E(N-1)$$

Then we expand out the formula we just came up with for $E(N)$ and use it for $E(N-1)$ also. The result looks long, but is still conceptually simple. So here is the full formula for $\Delta E(N)$:

$$\Delta E(N) = \left[C \times \frac{(1+R)^N - (1+RC)^N}{(R-RC)} + E(1+R)^N \right]$$
$$- \left[C \times \frac{(1+R)^{N-1} - (1+RC)^{N-1}}{(R-RC)} + E(1+R)^{N-1} \right]$$

Oh my gosh. Thank goodness for computers. Now we just plug these results into our regular FI formula to get FI(N). Here is the compact version:

$$FI(N) = \frac{\Delta E(N)}{TBI(N)} \times \frac{R - I}{R} \times (1 - ETR)$$

And here is the full load:

$$FI(N) = \left(\left[C \times \frac{(1+R)^N - (1+RC)^N}{(R-RC)} + E(1+R)^N \right] \right.$$
$$\left. - \left[C \times \frac{(1+R)^{N-1} - (1+RC)^{N-1}}{(R-RC)} + E(1+R)^{N-1} \right] \right) /$$
$$TBI(1+TBIR)^N \times \frac{R - I}{R} \times (1 - ETR)$$

Sheesh, man. That's a big formula. Well, like I said, don't worry too much about the details of the math. You see the concepts and you know there is no hocus pocus going on. Just as with FI, there is no opinion or bias in computing FI(N). Punch in the numbers and out will come the results. Want to know where you will be in ten years with your FI? Punch in the inputs and compute FI(10) and you will have it.

Since we can now project FI into the future, we can easily determine your projected FI date. All we do is project out year after year for FI(N) until we get a result of FI(N) $\geq$ 100. That point in time is your FI date. The date at which your FI finally surpasses 100.

The FI date and FI(N) are projections. You don't want to build your plan on projections. You want to build your plan on your current FI. On the here and now. FI(N) and your FI date are just supporting information and motivational tools. Your focus should still be on increasing your FI as much as possible in the current time period. The best way to draw your FI date closer is to increase your current FI right now. To compute FI(N), we need eight inputs:

R: Market Rate
I: Inflation Rate
E: Current Equity Amount
TBI: Current Time-Based Income
TBIR: TBI Rate of Change
C: Current Investment amount
RC: Investment Rate of Change
ETR: Equity Tax Rate

Let's look at some examples to see how FI changes over time for various scenarios using the formula for FI(N). If you are following the drone path, you may have inputs like the following:

R (Market Rate)	0.1
I (Inflation Rate)	0.03
E (Starting Equity)	0
TBI (Starting TBI)	$100,000.00
TBIR (TBI Rate of Change)	0.03
C (Starting Annual Investment)	$5,000.00
RC (Investment Rate of Change)	0.03
ETR (Equity Tax Rate)	0

This is someone starting out making $100,000K per year and saving 5% of that income. I've been saying that people like this are on the 40 or 50 year plan. Let's see what this person's FI date will be. If I plug in the numbers, I determine that this person will hit FI=100 in 47.25 years. Yep, sounds like the 40 to 50 year plan to me. Nice to see that the formula confirms our expectations. So, if you follow someone's advice to save 5% of your income, you better put part of your investment in Geritol because you are going to need some. Most folks don't really get rolling on a financial plan until their mid to late twenties. At a 5% savings pace, that means this person is going to be well into their seventies when they finally become financially independent. Thanks, but no thanks. I want a better plan.

I never said being a financial gladiator would be easy. You are going to have to get really aggressive to see improvements to your FI projections. Let's keep everything the same except for the savings rate. A financial gladiator will not follow a fixed savings rate. He will save as much as he can as early as he can. But, for comparison, let's say he was able to save 30% instead of the 5% we just did for the drone. The inputs to the FI(N) formula now look like this:

R (Market Rate)	0.1
I (Inflation Rate)	0.03
E (Starting Equity)	0
TBI (Starting TBI)	$100,000.00
TBIR (TBI Rate of Change)	0.03
C (Starting Annual Investment)	$30,000.00
RC (Investment rate of change)	0.03
ETR (Equity Tax Rate)	0

And the result is that the FI date will drop from 47.25 years all the way down to 21 years. Yes, 30% is a lot more than 5%, but we are talking about more than 25 extra years of freedom. I don't hear many financial gurus recommending a 30% savings rate. But I recommend it. I recommend even higher if you can find a way to do it. Absolutely. Yes, it is going to require living a lifestyle which consumes less income for 21 years, but isn't it worth it to live freely and have control of your time? Can't you find other ways to enjoy life along the way while saving 30% or more of your income?

One more example here. Let's say that you start off with a 30% savings rate. But you are motivated and don't want to wait 21 years. So you find ways to contribute more than 30% each year. You get passive income sources. Or you find new ways to cut expenses. One way or another, you improve on your investment rate by 5% each year. In my inputs, that means that the RC will exceed the inflation rate by 5%. Let's set the RC to 8%:

R (Market Rate)	**0.1**
I (Inflation Rate)	0.03
E (Starting Equity)	0
TBI (Starting TBI)	$100,000.00
TBIR (TBI Rate of Change)	0.03
C (Starting Annual Investment)	$30,000.00
RC (Investment rate of change)	0.08
ETR (Equity Tax Rate)	0

If you run the numbers with those inputs, then you will get your FI to 100 in less than 16 years. That's just amazingly superior to the drones' 47 year plan. No comparison whatsoever. Yes, the gladiator plan is challenging. It takes effort. It takes commitment. But it's a life changer. You'd be financially free more than 30 years before the 5% drone. 30 years!

Let me just compare this to what most financial planners do. They will pick some date and some number out in the future to set as your target. Then they will work backwards to today to determine how much you need to save to meet that goal. But consider that we are using estimates here. The farther out we project using those estimates, the less accurate our results will be. The traditional planner does two projections. First he projects forward to get the target, then he projects backward to get the current savings rate. Both of those projections are over the duration of the entire plan. In other words they are of maximum duration for the problem at hand.

Now consider the FI projection. The FI projection uses estimates too. But it uses those estimates far more efficiently. We start with today. Then we project forward one year at a time using FI(N). The higher N gets, the more reliant we are on our estimates. So FI(2) should be more accurate than FI(30). But even FI(30) is computed by using the estimates in only one forward pass. And that forward pass is made over as short a duration as possible. This completely blows the doors off of the tools that the traditional planner uses.

So, here is my advice as far as using these FI projections. I think it's really neat that we can do them. It gives us a glimpse into the future. An expectation of when we might be able to declare victory. And, even though the FI metric projections are far superior to the traditional projections, use them for what they are. Projections. Estimates. They are only as good as the estimated rates within them. There is no guarantee. I certainly think you should use them, but you must keep them in perspective. I suggest that you compute your FI date each month along with your FI. It's great motivation. But don't let it get you down if it turns out to be far off in the future. Just work on your FI for the current month. The more you do that, the more you will draw that date closer. If your FI date is close in time, then great. Use that as a big motivator to get over the last hurdle. Put that FI date behind you as soon as possible.

CHAPTER 7 KEYNOTES

1. Your FI Date is the date when your FI hits 100%

2. We can use math to project your FI

3. Do what you can to draw your FI date closer in time

CHAPTER 8
MONTHLY MEETINGS

"History does not long entrust the care of freedom to the weak or timid."

~Dwight D. Eisenhower

The FI metric system is a framework. It's a great framework, but it's not a complete financial plan. What the framework calls for is for *you* to develop your own financial plan within the framework. To do this, you will be conducting monthly meetings. During the meetings you will use lessons learned from the past, combined with your current financial information, to devise a new plan for each upcoming month. These meetings should not be a major ordeal. They should be fairly short. Less than an hour most of the time.

If you are married or have other persons involved in your financial life, then this is the time to get them involved. You need to let them know that you are working on getting your freedom and that you want their participation and assistance. The FI metric cycle looks like this:

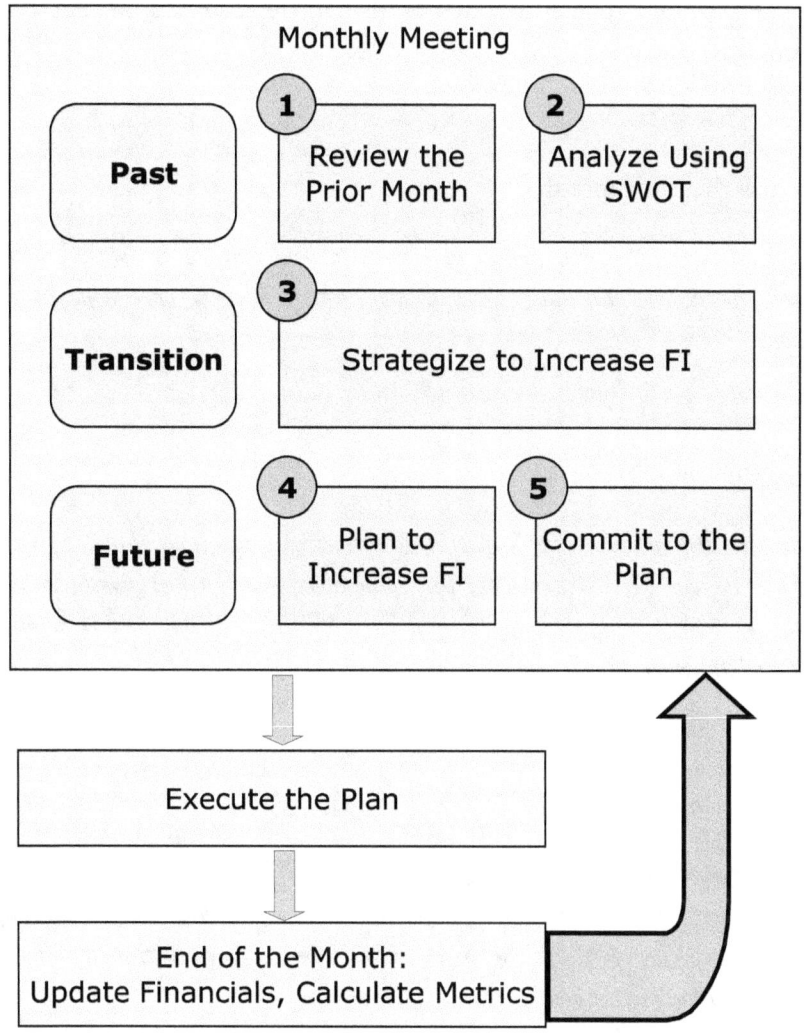

During each monthly meeting, you will learn as much as you can from the past. You will use that information to strategize about ways to increase your FI. The strategizing step transitions from the past to the future. Once you have your strategies in place then you start looking toward the future. You develop a plan to increase your FI for next month. Finally, you commit to the plan. When the meeting is done, you put the plan into action. You work the plan for the month and then rinse and repeat.

The meetings focus on your FI. All five steps should be centered around it.

1. Review the prior month

You should review the prior month in regards to how your FI is doing. Did it increase, decrease or stay flat? Does it look like you could have done better somehow?

2. Analyze using SWOT

The analysis step looks at your Strengths, Weaknesses, Opportunities and Threats in regards to your FI. What was the best thing about your FI last month. What was the worst. What opportunities do you have to increase it this coming month. What might threaten it?

3. Strategize to increase FI

The strategy session puts everything on the table. What are your options for increasing your FI in the upcoming month. Extra expense cutting, moving investments, working more, finding passive income. Put all possible strategies on the table and think out of the box.

4. Plan to Increase FI

Now that you have a bunch of information and strategies to work with, come up with a plan. The plan should focus on increasing your FI in the very next month. Set a specific goal. Pick your best strategies to increase equity growth and FI. Formalize it and document it. The plan adapts and changes every month.

5. Commit to the Plan

Document the plan, print it out and sign off on it. The commitment will keep you on track.

This is where the rubber hits the road. If the framework is going to be successful for you, then you need to be serious about these meetings. I suggest actually documenting the five steps of the meeting and keeping those meeting minutes around so you can review them in the future. Lets dig into each of the five steps in detail. All you have to do is put together a form with five sections that allow you to write in a narrative for each of the five steps. Something like the following:

Monthly FI Meeting March 2011

Jack and Diane

MEETING NOTES:

1. Review of the Prior Month

2. SWOT Analysis

3. Strategies to Increase FI

4. Plan for Next Month

Agreement of Commitment Jack: _____

Agreement of Commitment Diane: _____

If you don't document all of this, then you won't remember what you were thinking a year or two in the future. Getting it all down on paper will help when you start looking backward into your financial past for lessons learned. It will make you a better planner going forward. Lets dig further into each section.

Step 1: Review the prior month: At the end of each month, you will be updating your financial statements and calculating your metrics. This will include updating your balance sheet, computing your equity growth, your FI and FI date. You should also update and document other things from the prior month that might help increase your FI. This may include a detailed breakdown of expenses. Or details of investment returns. Whatever you think is worth looking at that might help with your plan for next month. You need to do all of that before you start your meeting. Once all of that information is available, you are ready to conduct your monthly FI meeting.

The first step in the meeting is to review the information from last month. This review is not an in-depth analysis. It's more of a high level overview of how you feel about the month that just passed. What were the big accomplishments. What were the big disappointments. Is the plan financially effective for you? Is it emotionally effective? The review should give a brief description of how you feel your plan went last month and how you feel about the process.

Step 2: SWOT Analysis: A SWOT analysis is a detailed breakdown of your strengths, weaknesses, opportunities, and threats. Not just what happened last month, but everything that is available to you now. This is where you need to get really detailed about things. Now that you have done a high level overview of last month, you are in position to really find the nitty gritty about how things went and how they can go in the future. What strengths did you have? Maybe you replaced an expensive hobby with one that is more affordable but just as enjoyable. Maybe you cut an unneeded expense. Maybe you went extreme couponing and cut your grocery bill buy $500 for the month. Maybe you had some strong investment returns. Maybe you worked some extra hours and used the money to pay off debt. Maybe you added some kind of passive income source. Just list out all of the good stuff so that you know what is working for you.

Likewise, list out the weaknesses. Did you go on a spending spree that was unneeded? Did you buy something that didn't really add any enjoyment to your life? Did you run into some big unexpected expense that you should have known about but did not plan for? Maybe you have some investments that performed poorly. Maybe you have a business that had a bad month. List it all out so you can become aware of the weaknesses for the month completed.

Next list out all of the opportunities you may take advantage of in the upcoming month. A good source for these are in the strengths and weaknesses you just listed. Do you have the opportunity to eliminate a weakness or build on a strength. If so, take advantage of that opportunity. List out every opportunity you can think of to increase your FI.

The final step in the SWOT analysis is to list out any threats. Scan out over your financial horizon and think of any threats that may be coming your way. Are there any expenses coming down the pipeline. DMV renewals, insurance payments or anything like that. Also consider your overall financial health. Do you have enough liquidity? Are your assets diversified enough? Do you have enough insurance? These are all potential threats to your financial health. You might want to use a SWOT chart for this. You can come up with your own or find one on the internet or on my website. SWOT analysis is commonly used in business and marketing. It's also a great tool for financial planning. Here is one sample of a SWOT chart:

Jack and Diane, SWOT Chart March 2011

STRENGTHS	WEAKNESSES
OPPORTUNITIES	THREATS

Step 3. Strategize to increase your FI: Now you have to transition from backward looking to forward looking thinking. Here you need to come up with possible strategies that you can include in your plan this coming month. Don't worry if it's not feasible to do all of these strategies, just list them all out. Whatever you list is a candidate for inclusion in your plan. You may execute some of the strategies in the next month and others sometime in the future. Get your mind flowing on things you can do to increase your FI. One idea may lead to another.

There are all kinds of things you can do to increase FI. Cut your phone bill, cut your cable bill, work some overtime, increase your 401K contribution, clip coupons, use a cash rebate credit card or find a better insurance rate on your car. The next chapter is dedicated to giving you some ideas on how to come up with gladiator strategies to increase your FI.

Step 4: Plan to increase your FI: Now you are going to select from all of the strategies that you put down in step 3. You may have more strategies than you can handle. Pick the ones you want to execute in the current plan. When you develop your plan for the upcoming month, be aggressive. Remember all of the things that we've gone over in this book. Time is important and you shouldn't delay getting tough and serious about having an aggressive plan for each month. Don't put down an impossible plan, but put down the best plan that you can realistically get done.

Set a target goal for your FI for the upcoming month. Something higher than what you just measured for the previous month. Look through your SWOT analysis for strengths that you can build on and opportunities you can take advantage of. Anything that can make some marginal improvement to your FI is a step in the right direction. Even a tenth of a percent each month will help. But, be aggressive and focused.

This is no time to be a pawn or a drone. You need to let the gladiator out and get things going. Shoot for major accomplishments in each and every month. Consider your FI date. Each aggressive step you take here will draw that date closer and closer.

Step 5: Commit to the plan: This is symbolic but it's important to make sure that all of the parties involved are serious about following the plan. What a waste of effort all of this work will be if you don't get everyone to commit to follow the plan.

That's all there is to conducting a monthly FI metric meeting. Just go through the steps and get your plan in place for the month going forward. This shouldn't take long at all. Make it fun and interesting. Keep conducting the meetings and your FI will respond. After the meeting, the execution phase begins. You will go through the month and follow the plan and your FI will increase. But if an unplanned opportunity comes up to increase your FI, take advantage of it. Don't blindly follow the plan if something better happens during the month. That's drone thinking, not gladiator thinking.

What a great thing it would be if families would get together and conduct these meetings every month. One of the leading causes of the breakup of families due to divorce is money. Couples disagree about money issues and don't communicate well. This leads to frustration and anger. By meeting once a month to plan out your finances, you will both know where you stand. Just the act of preparing a monthly balance sheet will do wonders for communicating. Both spouses will know where they stand on things. Both will see how their habits are impacting their financial success. If you can work together on increasing your freedom and improving your finances, then you can strengthen your relationship.

Treat your knowledge of financial independence as if it's your own personal financial coach sitting on your shoulder. Let it guide you throughout the month. If you are mid month and some tempting purchase comes along, listen to your inner coach. Stop and consider what affect that the purchase will have on your FI.

CHAPTER 8 KEYNOTES

1. Review your finances every month

2. Learn from past performance

3. Strategize to increase FI

4. Plan the next month and commit

CHAPTER 9
GLADIATOR STRATEGIES

"The longer you wait for the future, the shorter it will be."

~Loesje

There are lots of ways to develop your own detailed financial plan. The FI metric system is a highly structured framework that helps you to make sure your financial plan is effective and efficient. It does that by focusing on your FI and adapting to changes as needed. Whatever plan of action you take, remember to focus on increasing FI and doing it as soon as possible. That said, you have great freedom in choosing the strategies that you want to follow.

The first strategy that you should follow is to put everything on the table. Don't put blinders on and exclude possible strategies because you are not familiar with them. Don't focus only on paying off debt. Don't focus only on earning more income or on earning better income. You need to use all means available to you to increase your equity growth and your FI. I like Dave Ramsey, but he focuses too much on debt. I like Suze Orman, but she focuses too much on credit scores and retirement accounts. I like Jim Cramer, but he is all about stocks. You should listen to those people, but keep in mind that they are only giving you a small piece of the puzzle. It's a big financial world out there. You need to consider any method that will increase your FI. It's all about equity growth. Strategy sessions should be like brainstorming sessions. Think out of the box. Do lots of reading. Research on the internet. There is an infinite supply of ideas that you can turn into strategies to increase your financial freedom. As I said in the intro of this book, the FI metric system is not a detailed plan, it is a framework. It's up to you to come up with your own strategies for equity growth. You need to find your own path.

Even though there are an infinite number of strategies that you can use to increase your FI, they all come down to only a few major types:

1. Cutting Expenses
2. Increasing Income Quality
3. Increasing Income Quantity
4. Equity Management

You may notice that I don't list paying off debt as a strategy. The idea of paying off debt has been way overdone. Too many people get the "pay off debt" blinders on and forget about everything else. Paying off debt is only a result of doing the four things that I mentioned above. You can't pay off debt unless you do one of those things first. In order to have the means to pay off debt, you must first cut expense or increase income or get returns on your equity. The actual act of paying off debt isn't really very significant. The significant factor is having the means to do it. It's becoming quite the financial planning sensation to focus on paying off debt. Seems like with the recent collapse of asset values that's all advisors want to focus on. I don't pay much attention to it myself. Of course I want a nice clean balance sheet. Of course it's good to pay off debt. Of course it's good to be debt free. But that's just a beginning. It's not the finish line. It's not the focus of good system. If you focus on paying off debt then you get to an artificial finish line which is really just a starting line.

When people scream, "I'm debt freeeeee!" I say, "So what?" Big frickin' deal. Debt free by itself just means you are starting at zero. What else do you have on your balance sheet, Mr. Debt Free? You can file Chapter 7 bankruptcy and become debt free. Is that the formula for success? If you have no assets on your balance sheet, then you still have a looooong way to go. You'll be debt free and driving in to your wage slave job for quite some time to come. Go ahead and have your celebration, but keep it in context. Being debt free is not the goal. I'd rather have a small amount of debt with $2M in assets than to be debt free. Equity is the important thing and that is what the FI metric system focuses on. So, while some planners put the standard for success at "I'm debt freeee!", let's shoot higher. Much higher. Let's settle for nothing less than true financial freedom. FI=100 ASAP. That's the standard for success that we are shooting for. Debt free is just a bump in the road. Paying off debt is not a strategy. It's a side effect.

1. Cutting Expenses. This is the ancient financial planning tool. It remains very powerful today. It's particularly effective in the FI metric system because every expense you cut leads directly to an increase in equity of the same amount. Dollar for dollar, cutting expenses adds to equity growth. Cut your expenses for the month by $500 and your equity growth for the month must increase by $500 accordingly. It's a 100% return on the effort.

Back in 1998, Thomas J. Stanley wrote a book titled *The Millionaire Next Door*. In it, he explained how his research showed that millionaires were most often created through frugality and discipline. That should make perfect sense because expenses are the source of our dependence on TBI. Without expenses we would already be free. When you incur an expense, it is a 100% loss on those funds in regards to FI. A total and complete waste. So cutting expenses is a powerful way to increase FI. I could calculate out how many thousands you would save over the years by giving up Starbucks coffee, but I don't think you will really gain anything from that. It's up to you how much you cut and where you make those cuts. The list of possibilities in nearly endless. You can carpool, brown bag your lunch, turn off the cable TV, re-shop your insurance, restructure your debt, cut your tax bill, eat at home more often, lower your cell phone bills and on and on. People write entire books on the subject of frugality and cost cutting.

Expense cutting might not be my strongest point. I'm a really busy guy and the thought of going to some of the extremes that I hear people go to is beyond my level of tolerance. You will never find me making my own laundry softener. I'm not knocking it. It's just that it's not for me. More power to you if you can do stuff like that. There's a new TV show about extreme couponing. These folks are pretty amazing. They can go into a store and buy $800 worth of groceries and come out paying less than $10 dollars. That's pretty cool. But if you watch closely you'll see that these people spend a lot of time getting prepared for their shopping sprees. Sometimes as much time as a full-time job would take. When I look at it in those terms, then it's clearly not worth it to me. I can earn a lot more than $800 for a week's worth of work.

I look for reasonable ways to cut costs. If something is costly but gives no great benefit to my life, then of course I want to cut it out of the budget. We all have our limits on cost cutting. We can't live our lives without incurring some kind of expenses. I think someone who is really on fire to become financially free should be cutting pretty deep. Remember that cost cutting is highly potent because any expense is going to be a 100% loss against your FI.

You can look at cost cutting through FI colored glasses by figuring out how much each expense reduces your FI. Let's say my cable TV is costing me $150 per month. If my TBI is $7,500 per month, then I can compute how much that cable TV is restricting my financial freedom. Just plug in your expense into this formula:

$$\text{FI CHANGE} \; = \; \frac{\text{EXPENSE}}{\text{TBI}} \times \frac{R - I}{R} \times (1 - \text{ETR})$$

So if I use the standard deflator of .7 and an ETR of .25 I can see that the $150 expense would change my FI by

$$\text{FI CHANGE} = 150/7{,}500 \times .7 \times .75 = 1.05\%$$

In other words, the cable TV eats up about 1% of my financial freedom. Is it worth it? Depends how important it is to you and on how intense you are on getting your freedom. If you are intense about it, you might be able to increase your financial independence by 5% or 10% just by making a few cuts to similar things that don't add much value to your life.

Cost cutting can do wonders over the long haul. But, it's hard work and it takes discipline. If you are into extreme cost cutting, then great. Maybe you can make a huge improvement to your FI. Most of us are only willing to go so far. That means if we want to get our FI going, then we need to do something with our income. Cut as deep as you reasonably can and then look to ways to improve the quantity and quality of your income.

2. Increase Income Quality. Now for my personal favorite: increasing the quality of your income. What I mean by this is that we should seek income that is not time based. Or at least not totally time based. The more passive the income is, the better. If it requires our time then it's of low quality. Having a lot of high quality (passive) income is great. It's the most rewarding of the four major categories because it happens without needing a lot of ongoing effort on our part. You may have to put in a lot of effort upfront, but once your income source is rolling, it generates income on its own. This is the kind of income you would get from rents, royalties, business sales and so on. Often this is entrepreneurial income.

Unfortunately, it's hard to come by this income. Not everyone is going to be able to succeed at generating a lot of passive income. If you can do it, great. It's the fast lane to financial independence. But it also carries a lot of risk. You might invest a lot of resources in making an attempt to gain some passive income and come up completely empty. Most business startups will fail. Most attempts at royalty income from books, music or what have you also generate minimal returns. Even if you do succeed at it, sometimes that passive income stream ends up being a whole lot of work.

Having said all of that, I am a big fan of entrepreneurship. I am an entrepreneur myself. The FI metric system works just great with the entrepreneurial mind. This isn't a book about starting an internet business or becoming a real estate tycoon. But I think you should do yourself a favor and keep the passive income route on the table for yourself. Read lots of books on startup businesses and true millionaire success stories. Listen to other successful entrepreneurs and learn from them. Just don't fall prey to the get rich quick gimmicks along the way. Reading and learning is one thing, but investing in someone else's scheme is risky. Be cautious.

I've found that there are some great resources available online for people seeking to improve the quality of their income. I'll mention a few of those sources here because I've learned a lot from them. First off I'd like to mention a guy by the name of Pat Flynn. Pat is a young entrepreneur who lost his job due to a downturn in the economy. But rather than wallow in unemployment misery, Pat has made the best of it. He's become a top notch web marketer who knows a lot about blogging, search engine optimizations, podcasting and affiliate income streams. Put simply, he is an expert on passive income generated on the internet. Best of all, he openly shares his techniques with anyone interested. Pat's blog is called *The Smart Passive Income Blog*. You can find his site at *http://www.smartpassiveincome.com*. He's got a great personal story and some great content on his site. Pat does something really interesting. He actually posts his income and expenses from his passive income activities on his website. I think that's one of the reasons he is so popular. He is showing people how he generates passive income and he is putting up the numbers to prove it. His latest report, as of the writing of this book, is for April 2011 where he posted over $40,000 of income for the month. In Pat's words "getting laid off was the best thing that ever happened to me." Sounds like a financial gladiator to me. He's not waiting for his future to happen, he's making it happen. Do yourself a favor and check out the Smart Passive Income site.

There are lots of great resources available on the internet. Let me mention just one more. Jamie Tardy has a site called *The Eventual Millionaire.* Jamie had gone to a great school and had launched a career making six figures. But she found herself hating her job and racking up debt. In my terms, she was on the drone's path of life. Work at a job that you don't like and squirrel away some of your income in hopes of a better day forty or fifty years down the road. Jamie decided that the drone path was not for her. In 2006, she turned into a financial gladiator and paid off a mountain of debt. She was able to quit the job that she hated and now she helps entrepreneurs to improve their businesses. What I absolutely love about her site is that she interviews millionaires from various industries. You can learn a lot by listening in on these interviews. I don't know how she gets these interviews, but it's to our benefit that she makes them available to us for free. I've listened to pretty much every one of her interviews with millionaires. Not a single one of those folks got to where they are by following the drone's path. Every single one is a financial gladiator. Each one making it happen, not waiting for it to happen. A lot of the interviews are consistent with what Thomas J. Stanley had found in his research. Millionaires are often frugal. Jaime interviewed Dan Nainan who is a really interesting guy who made the transition from engineer to successful comedian. He is now a millionaire and is doing what he loves. But, he still lives a very frugal life consistent with the findings that Stanley wrote about years ago.

Millionaires may be frugal, but the vast majority of the millionaires that Jamie has interviewed got to where they are by generating income from some kind of business. A good business is one that exhibits one of two traits. Either it generates a very large income, or it generates passive income. These are common themes among millionaires. If you want to hear about success stories and winning strategies right from the millionaires themselves, then check out Jamie's podcast and website by going to *http://www.eventualmillionaire.com*.

Starting a business is great, but it's not for everyone. There are other ways to generate passive income streams. Real estate is one of those ways. Maybe it's not as quick and exciting as creating a new business, but you can generate some significant streams of income from rental property. We've just come through a nasty decline in real estate so it's not in vogue now. Despite the fact that a lot of people have had bad experiences with real estate recently, it may be a great time to invest. Interest rates and prices are way down which makes for a great combination.

Don't limit yourself to just those sources that I have mentioned. Go out and find your own great passive income streams. By increasing the quality of your income, you will be taking a big step to improving your FI. Not only will you increase your FI, but you will also diversify your financial resources. Relying solely on the stock market and bond market for your income is drone thinking. By finding creative streams of passive income, you are diversifying your financial resources. Maximize the quality of your income and you will get the double benefit of increasing your FI and increasing your diversification.

3. Increase the Quantity of Your Income. Increasing the quantity of your income just means earning more dollars. If you can get a pay raise or change careers or do something else to kick up your income, then you can use that extra income to turbocharge your FI. Of course it will only work if you use that income properly. You will need to put that new extra income toward your equity growth for it to contribute to your freedom. If you don't, it will actually *lower* your FI.

The strategies you employ here are up to you. Maybe you need some education to earn a degree or credential to juice up your income. Or maybe you need to work longer hours and dedicate that extra income to equity growth. If you are a single income family, maybe it's time to kick that hubby or wife in the butt and go dual income. Maybe it's time to negotiate an increase with your employer. Find a way to make yourself worth more to your employer first, and then seek an increase.

Increasing your income can lead to increases in your FI. Just don't fall into the trap of becoming dependent on that increasing income. Reserve it for equity growth and increases to FI. Consider this. Let's say Jack starts off with an FI around 30%. Ignore taxes and inflation again. Let's say he has equity growth of $3,000 month and TBI of $10,000 per month.

$$FI = 3,000 / 10,000 = 30\%$$

Now let's say Jack comes into an extra $1,000 of income each month. Here is case one where he gets that extra $1,000 from TBI and spends it all. So his TBI goes up by $1,000 but his equity growth stays the same. Here is the resulting FI:

$$FI = 3,000 / 11,000 = 27\%$$

Since Jack has squandered his extra $1,000, his FI actually goes down by 3%. This is how dependence on TBI creeps into your life. You get a raise and then you go buy stuff because you have "extra" money. The result is that you become dependent on that raise. You have made yourself more of a wage slave.

Now consider if Jack puts the $1,000 to good use and increases his equity growth by the full $1,000 per month. In this case, his TBI goes up by $1,000 but so does his equity growth. His FI numbers look like this:

$$FI = 4,000 / 11,000 = 36\%$$

Much better. Now he has used the raise to crank up his FI. That extra $1,000 raise is giving him a boost of 6% in his freedom. This should be your objective when increasing the quantity of your income. Put it to good use and it will increase your FI.

Finally, if Jack could earn that $1,000 through passive income, he could do even better. In that case, his equity growth would increase, but his TBI would be the same. Here his numbers would be:

$$FI = 4,000 / 10,000 = 40\%$$

A whopping 10% jump for increasing both the quality and quantity of his income and applying that increase to equity growth.

So, do what you can to increase the quantity of your income. But, make sure that you don't fall into the trap of becoming dependent on that income. Use it to increase your equity growth and your FI.

4. Managing Your Equity. The FI metric system encourages equity growth. Once your equity starts rising, you better take steps to manage it properly. Do you have a credit card balance on a card that has a 19% interest rate, while at the same time you have a bunch of cash sitting in a bank account earning 2%? If so, you are not managing your equity well. You should always be on the lookout for situations like the one just mentioned because they are financial no-brainers. It makes no sense to pile up tons of cash or to invest in stocks while you have 19% credit card debt. You won't earn 19% in the market in the long run. And you take on risk for the 10% or so that you might earn. In contrast, the 19% on the credit card is guaranteed and there is no risk. Paying off that card will result in a 19% return and there is 0 risk. You can't get that anywhere else. You must take advantage of obvious equity restructuring like that.

Once the obvious stuff is done, it's up to you to decide what to hold on your balance sheet. Assets come in many flavors. Stocks, real estate, bonds, options, cash. Each asset should give you an appropriate return for the level of risk that it brings. The higher the risk, the higher the return you should demand. My suggestion is to stay fairly aggressive in investing as long as your FI is below 100. As your FI nears and passes 100, you can consider taking on less risk.

You should also manage your equity such that you maintain appropriate levels of liquidity and diversity. Liquidity is your ability to meet short-term demands. Don't go putting money into a retirement account if there is a chance that you need to pull it out early and get hit with a penalty. That's bad management. You should keep enough liquid assets available to meet your needs as appropriate for your situation. There is a saying in the investing world—"cash is trash." That's because cash earns little or no return. If you have too much of your equity in cash, then you are not putting it to work. But having too little can leave you in a pinch and cause you to make some really bad decisions. It's a balancing act.

Some planners recommend three months' worth of expenses. Some recommend eight months or a year. I think it's ridiculous for a planner to recommend a certain liquidity level across the board. You need to look at your own situation and decide how much of your equity you need to keep in cash. Don't follow some advisor's across-the-board suggestion. That's drone thinking again. If you have been in your job for ten years and the position is stable, then you need less liquidity than someone who has been in their position for a year. If you have two stable incomes in your home, then you need less liquidity than a home with one income. Maybe three months is good enough, maybe you need eight months or a year. Look at your situation and decide for yourself. You know your situation better than any advisor.

Diversity is important too. Don't just diversify your investment across different stocks and different industries. Make sure that you are diversified across asset classes too. If you are well diversified in the stock market and the entire stock market gets hammered then your entire equity pool gets hammered. Put some into other assets like bonds or real estate. The more diversity the better.

The strategies you employ to increase your FI are yours to choose. Keep an open mind and keep everything on the table. Make sure that you manage your equity and maintain adequate liquidity and diversity.

CHAPTER 9 KEYNOTES

1. Cut expenses

2. Increase the quantity of your income

3. Increase the quality of your income

4. Mange your equity

5. Learn from others

6. Develop your own strategies

CHAPTER 10
FORKS IN THE ROAD

"It's not hard to make decisions when you know what your values are."

~ Roy Disney

Throughout your life you are going to face countless financial decisions. Buy a house or rent? Roth IRA or traditional IRA? Go to school and get a degree or start a business? Invest in Microsoft, Google or Apple? All of those decisions are financial forks in the road. You can't take both paths so you have to choose one and go forward. Those decisions are what will determine your financial future. Make good choices and you can look forward to financial independence. Take the wrong fork in the road and you will pay for it later.

When you get to a financial fork in the road, pull out the best tool that you have to help make that decision. Pull out the FI metric. Use it to guide your decision. Look at the options that lie before you and select the one that will increase your FI the most. You need to turn the FI metric into your own financial coach. It needs to speak to you in these times of decision making.

This is something you need to work at. You need to develop this decision making skill. We all make mistakes with our finances. The best we can do is to minimize the mistakes that we make and to deal with the results as best as we can. I've learned from some of the poor choices that I've made in the past. I won't make those bad choices again because now I would look at them through FI metric colored glasses. I don't make financial decisions without considering their impact on my freedom.

As you start to follow the FI metric system, you will become familiar with how your financial decisions effect your FI. You will see that taking on debt will create a liability on your balance sheet. Accordingly, that will reduce your equity. You'll see that there is an interest expense associated with debt. And that interest expense prevents you from adding to your equity. This results in a lower FI. By seeing these effects, you will get more proficient at making better financial decisions. This is how the FI metric works as a motivational tool. You should make every financial decision within the context of how it affects your FI.

If you use the metric as just a cold, meaningless number, then you are missing the point of the whole system. The metric should be used as a catalyst for change. If there is no change in your financial behaviors, then what's the point of the system? To get full benefit of the metric, you need to use it to guide your decision making process. Do that and you will really be putting the system to its intended purpose.

I don't think you need a whole lot of rah-rah coaching to convince you to use the metric as a motivational tool. If you just see it month after month, then it will create its own motivation within your mind. Nobody likes to be called a wage slave. If you look down and see an FI of 10, then that means you are 90% wage slave. This is a form of negative reinforcement. Things aren't going well so you need a shock to get you moving. Knowing that you are 90% wage slave is pretty darn good motivation for you. Better than any rah-rah speech I can give you.

It works the other way too. Once you see your FI start to grow, it motivates you to crank it up even higher. Your FI is at 75% so you only have 25% to go. This is positive reinforcement. Good financial decisions lead to a higher FI and you see the effects of your work paying off.

The FI metric is to finances as a scale is to a weight loss program. When you try to lose weight, a scale plays an important role. Just the act of getting on the scale and weighing in creates its own motivation. If it comes up a bad number, then you know you are on the wrong track. You need to change your diet and your exercise. That's negative reinforcement in action. If you did shed some pounds, then you know what you are doing is working. Positive reinforcement tells you to continue on the program. By seeing how your decisions cause a certain result on the scale, you are able to modify your decision making process. You start to realize what foods you can and can't eat. What exercise program is and is not working. You are using the results on the scale to guide your decision making process. You hit a fork in the road. Should I eat that triple decker bacon cheeseburger or should I have a salad? You know which one is going to get the best result on the scale.

Likewise, you will start to realize which financial decisions are increasing your FI and which are not. You will learn how to choose between the financial triple decker bacon cheeseburger and the salad. Does it really make sense for me to buy a $32,000 brand new vehicle and to do it on credit? Or should I buy a $10,000 used vehicle and pay cash? Do I need 600 cable TV channels? Or can I turn the whole darn thing off, do something better with my time and save a hundred bucks a month? Look at it through how it will affect your FI and then make your decision.

Of course, making the right decision is not always easy. Even if you know the ramifications, you might not make the right decision. I know the triple decker cheeseburger is bad, but I still want it. I know the

$32,000 car is bad, but I still want it. It's up to each of us as individuals to make the right choice. Consider your choice carefully. With weight loss, the repercussion is fitness or fatness. With finances, the repercussion is freedom or slavery. Is the $32,000 car really worth making yourself more of a wage slave? Is it really worth reducing your freedom for a car? Hey, it's a free world so maybe it is worth it for you. But not for me. I'll choose freedom. If a car is going to make me a wage slave, then you can keep the car.

I think that the opening quotation for this chapter says it very well. Roy Disney said, "It's not hard to make decisions when you know what your values are." Your financial decisions will be driven by your values. If your values are strong, then it becomes easy to make the right decision. What is important to you in life? Is it more stuff? Fancier stuff, bigger stuff? Is it having status symbols of wealth? Or is freedom more important to you? At the heart of the FI metric system is a value system. One that values freedom very highly. Much more so than being filthy rich and buying everything you lay eyes on. The FI metric system pops up at every fork in the road and reminds you of your values. Freedom over stuff. True independence over phony status. A strong balance sheet over fancy cars and a big house.

This is what separates gladiators from drones. Gladiators have a solid value system with freedom way at the top of the list. Ahead of everything else. Drones like comfort. They like stuff more than freedom. When you buy "stuff," whether it's a fancy new car or a big house or an 84-inch flat screen TV, you need to look at the exchange for what it really is. It's not an exchange of money for stuff. It's an exchange of stuff for freedom. That fancy car erodes your independence. That flat screen TV chains you to your paycheck. Money is just the conduit through which you make that exchange. You're not giving up money for that thing you are buying, you are giving up your independence. Whenever you face a financial choice, pause and consider what it is doing to your freedom. Run the numbers and figure out what it will do to your FI. Let that guide your decision.

If you still want to make that purchase after viewing it in this context, then go ahead. It must be very important to you. But don't make financial decisions without first considering their effect on your freedom.

When you go out into the retail world, it's a completely one-sided affair. Business people are smart. Marketers will try everything at their disposal to get you to buy their product. They will make it look sexy. They are masters at their craft. They can make a frickin' flashlight look sexy. Somehow they figure out a way to make whatever they are selling look good to you. They will put you into a carefree environment that encourages you to spend. They will use peer pressure to make you want things you don't need. They will use your fear to make you think you need things that are really not important. They'll use your love for your kids or your spouse against you. It's them against you. The playing field is tipped heavily in their favor.

Don't go in unarmed or you will lose. Learn the power of "No." I have developed that awesome power over the years. I don't have any difficulty telling people "No" anymore. When I come to a fork in the road, I just consider the fact that my freedom is at stake. My freedom versus their glitzy marketing. In my world, that doesn't just level the playing field, it tips it in my favor. All of a sudden that shiny thing that they are selling doesn't look so good. All of a sudden the tricks that they are trying to pull get exposed for what they are. I'm in control. They are groveling.

You have to approach this decision making ability as a skill. You will get better and better at it over time. Some slick salesperson will talk you into buying something. Then, after paying for it for months or years, you will realize you got snookered. But you will see the result and you will learn from it. Your ability to make good financial decisions will improve as you monitor your finances and your progress toward financial independence.

Strengthen your value system. Put freedom before stuff. If you adopt freedom as your highest value, then you will make sound financial decisions. When you get to a fork in the road, always, always consider your freedom, first.

CHAPTER 10 KEYNOTES

1. Your financial future is determined by the decisions you make today

2. Use your FI to guide your decision making

3. Know your values: Freedom before stuff

CHAPTER 11
PULLING THE PLUG

"In the truest sense, freedom cannot be bestowed; it must be achieved."

~Franklin Delano Roosevelt

When your FI hits 100, you need to use a little common sense. If it was 80 last month and it hits 110 this month then you have no business pulling the plug on your TBI. Give yourself some leeway. How much leeway is up to you. I'd say at a minimum to make sure that your FI hits at least the 100 mark for 18 months in row. That's a year and a half of proven financial independence so it's a pretty good sign that you are ready. This is a time when it makes sense to look at how durable your FI is. You are no longer in the accumulation stage of FI. You have worked hard to get your FI to 100 or higher and now you are heading into the stage of your life where you may want to rely on the equity and or passive income streams that you have accumulated.

You probably want to reallocate a chunk of your portfolio to some fixed income assets to give you more stable returns as you become reliant on them. You don't want to have 100% of your equity in the stock market when you decide to pull the plug on your current job.

You need to transition your equity into more stable assets. Things like bonds, or annuities. Do your research and talk with a knowledgeable expert who can help with this decision. Asset allocation is important at this stage of the process so you want to get it right before you claim victory over your TBI.

I haven't talked about Social Security or other sources of income that you might be able to rely on after you cut off your TBI. I don't include them in my planning because I don't want to be dependent on them. You never know what the government might do. They are currently talking about reducing benefits or means testing to keep the system going. My view is that if Social Security is there for me, fine, but I don't want rely on it. I don't include it when computing my FI.

If you want to include Social Security or other sources in your FI metric planning, it's very easy to do. Just lower your FI target. If you think Social Security will provide 20% of your income, then you can shoot for FI=80 instead of FI=100. If you are expecting some kind of pension other than Social Security, you can do the same. Just drop your target. For you it's not FI=100 ASAP, it's FI=80 ASAP. I have no problem with that.

Also, consider financial changes that might occur after you pull the plug. If you are leaving a job and not getting another one, what will you do about health insurance? It might cost more than what you are currently paying. If you think you will have higher costs after you pull the plug, then just raise your target. For you maybe it's FI=120 ASAP instead of FI=100 ASAP. Again, I am fine with that. This is your plan not mine. I'm just giving you the framework to work within. The FI metric assumes that everything will cost the same before and after pulling the plug. Likely you will have some costs that are higher and other costs that are lower than what you are paying before you quit your job. This is a good time to talk to a qualified advisor to make sure that the transition goes smoothly.

When you have no TBI, the FI metric doesn't work any longer.

Since TBI is in the denominator of the formula, a zero results in an undefined result. It basically represents infinity. That kind of makes sense. If you have no TBI, then you are infinitely free. Since you will have made yourself financially independent, all you have to do is monitor your equity over time. If your estimates are right, then it should basically keep up with inflation. It should let you pull out enough to maintain your current lifestyle year after year while still growing enough to keep up with inflation. Of course in practice things won't be that linear. You will have good years and bad years. But overall, your equity growth should be sufficient to fund your lifestyle AND to keep up with the pace of inflation.

Honestly, I think that by the time your FI reaches 100, you will have considerable financial knowledge of your own. You will have spent years increasing and managing your equity. You will have seen up markets and down markets. You will have done much research on your own to maximize your equity growth. My recommendation is to just be practical. Stay in charge of things, but get with a financial advisor and shift some your assets to more stable asset classes. Decide on your own if you should give yourself some FI padding. Maybe you should shoot for FI=110 and keep your job just a little longer. Hey, it's going to be more enjoyable at the office when you know that you can bail out anytime you want to.

But pulling the plug on your TBI does not necessarily mean that your income has to go down. It just means that you are not going to work for a paycheck anymore. Now that you are no longer dependent on your paycheck, you should follow your passions. Don't just pull the plug and do nothing. Go out and live. Start that business that you have always dreamed of. Not for the money, but for the joy of it. Stay engaged and make the most of your freedom.

As I am writing this book, I am in the fortunate position to have an FI near 100. I have some great passive income streams from software that I have written. I have been investing in stocks and real estate for over twenty years. All of that has put me into position to have the freedom to choose what I do with my time. But I have no intention to sit around and watch life go by. I plan on being more engaged than ever. I have more things going on in my life now than I have ever had before. But now, I get to pick and choose what I do with my time. I don't have to work on something solely for the money. If it's interesting and worthwhile, then I'm in. If it's a stupid project and it's all about the money, then I'll pass.

If I could give you some advice regarding pulling the plug on your own TBI, it would be two things. First, don't pull the plug too soon. Double and triple check your financial situation before you take any actions. Is your equity well diversified? Do you have significant liquid assets? Do you have solid streams of passive income? Make sure that you are completely squared away before you pull the plug. Secondly, before you pull the plug, make sure you know what you are going to do with yourself. You don't want to pull the plug and then find out that life is boring and dull. Make sure that you have a plan of action. Maybe you'll keep working, but you will work on different things. Things that you like. Or, maybe you will quit work all together and just pursue other interests. Either way, just make sure that you have a plan to follow.

CHAPTER 11 KEYNOTES

1. Adjust your FI target as appropriate before pulling the plug

2. Allocate your assets more conservatively before you start to rely on them

3. Get a proven track record of FI above your target before pulling the plug

CHAPTER 12
ENJOY THE JOURNEY

"As you walk down the fairway of life you must smell the roses, for you only get to play one round."

~Ben Hogan

There is certainly more to life than just finances. The FI metric system embraces that fact. The FImetric framework is not about getting rich. It's about taking control of your life and enhancing your freedom. More freedom brings more enjoyment. Tony Horton is a world famous fitness trainer. He created a fitness program called P90X that has gotten thousands of people into the best shape of their lives. Tony also wrote a book entitled *Bring It*. In his book he talks about the importance of "Feel Good Fitness." Not that fitness is easy or effortless. Nope, his fitness program is tough. It's a killer. His point isn't that it should be easy. His point is that you need to train your mind and adapt your fitness program so that you "Feel Good" about it. Otherwise, you won't stick with it.

And, so it goes with finances. You aren't going to stick with a financial program if it makes you miserable. And why the heck should you? You need to train yourself to make good financial decisions. But you need to do it in a way that makes you feel good about it. Don't sacrifice everything now so that you can feel good later. Make changes now that you can feel good about currently and in the future. When I talk about savings, I don't use the term sacrifice. Most planners would tell you that you need to "sacrifice" now so that you can have a better tomorrow. But I don't look at it that way. I would rather learn how to get pleasure from saving now. It's not sacrifice. It's my value system. I value freedom more than stuff. I value my time more than things. Saving is not a depressing thing, it's a positive thing.

The consumption smoothers definitely think that saving means that you are *sacrificing* something now and that you are somehow saddened as a result of that saving. They think that the only way for you to enjoy life is to spend, spend, spend. But that assumes a zero sum game. As if there is only so much joy in your life and that to gain joy, you need to spend and consume. How sad. What a terrible value system. I think you can get the best of both worlds. By saving now, you get the obvious benefits of compound growth and long-term financial success. But you can also gain immediately by knowing that you have more financial stability. You have more freedom. You have more control. You get a higher FI. And you get it now. You don't just benefit in the future. You also benefit immediately. This is what I mean when I say that you must enjoy the journey. Do not be miserable while you are working on your financial success. You have to enjoy the journey as well as the finish line.

Think of your work environment. Let's be honest here. Most people really don't like their jobs. Some people hate their jobs. If it weren't for the paycheck, they would not show up. If you are on the FI metric plan, then you already know that you have a pathway to reduce your dependency on that job. But you also know that it is going to take some time. While you are working on it, don't take on the attitude that you hate your job more and more because you are working so hard to reduce your dependency. Instead, use the fact that you are reducing your dependency on that job to bring back some joy into your life. Yeah, maybe you are still a wage slave while you are working your FI metric plan. But, you have a plan in place. And, with every month that passes, you get closer and closer to freedom. Let that progress put joy into your life today. Don't focus only on the finish line.

Back when I talked about the consumption smoothers, I said that consumption smoothing was nonsense and that you should ignore it and get your FI=100 ASAP. Consumption smoothers may be good economists, but they are horrible financial advisors. You see, they don't understand that saving and being financially disciplined today does not mean that you have to reduce your enjoyment of life. On the contrary, you should allow your laser focus on your FI to allow you to enjoy life today more than you ever have. It takes work. It takes effort. But with the right perspective, you can do it. You can have the best of both worlds. The consumption smoothers don't get it. They think that the only way to enjoy life is to consume. But a FI metric gladiator doesn't buy into that perspective. A FI metric gladiator doesn't derive his gratification from consumption. He or she derives it from working on freedom. It's that value system at work again. Freedom versus stuff. For the FI metric gladiator, freedom wins every time. You know what's important to you. You know where you are and you know where you are going.

You've no doubt heard the phrase "time is money." In our society it is more true than ever before. We see it everywhere. The exchange of time for money is the accepted norm of modern life. If you had to quantify life, how would you do it? The obvious answer is time. Time is really all we have. When our time ends, our life ends. Logically therefore, life is time. If you put these two phrases into math statements you get this:

$$LIFE = TIME$$
$$TIME = MONEY$$

Math and logic have a law called the transitive law. It says that if A=B and B=C, then A=C. If we apply the transitive law to the two statements I just made we get:

$$LIFE=TIME$$
$$TIME=MONEY$$
$$LIFE=MONEY$$
(by transitive law)

I don't know about you, but I find that unacceptable. It's repugnant to think that life is money. Yet that is the reality that we live with. That is the defacto condition that we are put into by modern society. I can't deny it. Every day, we exchange significant parts of our lives for money. This is simply the norm in our modern culture. It is the natural state of things that LIFE=MONEY. If you find it unacceptable, then you need to do something to change it.

It's terrible to say that life is all about money. We should work against being put into that state. There are two ways to break that last equality that says LIFE=MONEY. You can break the equality that says LIFE=TIME or you can break the equality that says TIME=MONEY. I think you should try to do both.

There are certainly lives that transcend time. There have been inspiring people that have done amazing and courageous things which far outlive the time span of their life. These people have found a way to make life more than time. A lot of people have given their lives so that people like you and I might have a chance to live free. In my view, these people have broken the link that defines life by time. Their lives are worth more than the sum of the time that they were given. But this book is not about helping you find a way to make your life exceed the time that you have been given. I will leave that to you. This book is about financial freedom. So the second statement TIME=MONEY is what we are trying to destroy. The entire book has discussed the goal of ridding yourself of dependence on time-based income. That is exactly what financial independence does. It says:

TIME < > MONEY

It says that your time is no longer equivalent to money. You no longer need to trade your time for money to meet your financial needs. You can elect to do with your time whatever you want. Maybe you will trade some for money. But not because you have to.

Let that bring enjoyment to you as you make your financial journey. Your journey will take work. It will take effort. It will take time. But enjoy it because every step on that journey means you are one step closer to saying that your life is not about money. One step closer to saying that your life transcends money. If I were just saving in order to let my money grow so that I could buy more stuff later, then I would agree with the majority and say that you need to "sacrifice" today for a better tomorrow. But that's not what we FI metric gladiators do. We don't save today so that we can buy more stuff in the future. We save today so that we can buy more freedom. So there is no sacrifice. We win today and in the future. We enjoy the journey along the way because it is a journey into freedom.

CHAPTER 12 KEYNOTES

1. You must enjoy life along the way

2. Life is more than money

3. Enjoy your increased freedom

CHAPTER 13
THE ROAD LESS TRAVELED

"Indecision becomes decision with time."

~Author Unknown

In chapter 10 I talked about Forks in the Road. Now it's decision time for you. Will you stick to the road you are currently on? Or are you ready to hop into the FI metric Bugatti sports car and take the road less traveled? Will you trust your future to the financial gurus who are suggesting the slow path? Or are you ready to grab the wheel yourself and take control of your own financial future? I suspect that those who decide to follow the FI metric system will be in the minority. Of course that disappoints me. I wish it would catch on like wildfire and change financial lives all over the world. But I'm a realist. Financial independence is not easy. I think there will be a small niche of people bold enough to decide to take the road less traveled. The FI metric road.

In this final chapter, I am going to compare the two roads. The conventional financial planning road versus the FI metric road. If you've already decided to adopt the FI metric system, then this chapter is strong reinforcement that you've made a great choice. If you are planning on sticking with the conventional approach, then this is my last shot to convince you that you are on the wrong path.

If there is a financial planning body that is considered to be the defining source of best practices, it would be the Certified Financial Planner Board of Standards. They are the respected authority on financial planning. I have recently submitted the FI metric to them for their review in hopes that they will consider adopting it as a best practice. We'll see how they respond. For now, the CFP® board publishes the following list of six best practices for financial planning:

1. Set measurable goals

2. Understand the effect of each financial decision

3. Re-evaluate your financial situation periodically.

4. Start planning as soon as you can

5. Be realistic in your expectations

6. Realize you are in charge

I certainly did not design the FI metric system with the goal of meeting those six best practices. But it turns out that the FI metric system nails each and every one. I think you will be hard pressed to find a plan that meets those best practices as well as the FI metric system does. To help you make your decision as to whether or not to follow the FI metric road, here is a comparison of my system versus the traditional drone/yuppie version of financial planning.

1. Set measurable goals: Helloooo! There is no way anyone can possibly claim to have a better system than FI metric when it comes to setting measurable goals. The entire system is centered around the idea of doing exactly that. Measure your FI every single month. Nobody else has this great metric to work with. It took an outsider to see this. The experts were too set in their ways. Yes, you should set measurable goals, absolutely. And the best measurable goal to set is financial independence. This is a great best practice and the FI metric system embraces it.

What does the traditional system give you as far as measurable goals. You're pretty much left on your own. I guess you can check the balance of your 401(k) every month. Or you can say that your measurable goal is making sure that you save 15% of your income. Then you can check your paycheck to make sure that you are really saving that much. But those measurable goals are laughable compared to the FI metric. No comparison whatsoever. FI metric wins hands down.

Maybe you are a debt free freak. So your measurable goal is to get your liabilities on your balance sheet down to zero. Hey, at least it's measurable. I give them credit for that. But the goal is faulty. Debt free is a bogus target to shoot for. What will you do when you reach that target? You'll yell, "I'm debt free!" and then you'll get into your car and go to work the next day because you are still dependent on your paycheck. The FI metric kicks the tar out of debt free.

So, in the battle of FI metric vs. Traditional, when it comes to setting measurable goals, FI metric is the clear and undisputed winner. Score: 1-0.

2. Understand the effect your financial decisions have on other financial issues:

I can't think of any better way to do this than to have a comprehensive metric that takes into account everything in your financial life. Every financial decision you make gets rolled into the metric. I've stressed the importance of making your financial decisions within the context of how it affects your FI. If you don't proactively consider the effect of your financial decisions, the FI metric will do it for you. Make a bad decision, it will show up in your FI. Make a good decision and your FI will rise. The FI metric gives both positive and negative reinforcement. Another home run for FI metric.

What about the traditional approach? I guess I would say it is mixed at best. Sometimes traditional planners get disciplined and look at the big picture of your financial plan. But often, they get blinders on and just focus on one thing. Paying off credit card debt, increasing your FICO score, picking the best stocks. It's easy for the traditional approach to hide the effects of your decisions on other parts of your financial life.

Again, FI metric wins. Current score: 2-0.

3. Re-evaluate your financial plan periodically: Yeah, how about continuously? The FI metric system calls for you to have monthly meetings to evaluate and plan your finances. But it also encourages you to make changes within a month whenever appropriate. FI metric is highly dynamic. Best practice met!

The traditionalists would prefer that you come in to their office and have them generate a glitzy financial plan for you. Who knows how much they will charge–$500 or $1,000, maybe. And how do you re-evaluate? Well, you go back in to the office in a year and get a new plan. And you pay another $500 or $1,000 again. It's terrible. It's designed around static ideas. It's great for the financial planners' revenues, but not so good for your financial freedom.

FI metric is way more dynamic than traditional. Hands down winner. Current score 3-0.

4. Start now: Heck, yes. The FI metric system sets as its goal FI=100 ASAP. Start now and do as much as you can as soon as you can. I stress the importance of time. I've proven how important time is by sharing the TVM formulas with you. The goal itself underscores how important time is. It says ASAP–AS SOON AS POSSIBLE. It encourages a sense of urgency and immediacy to get things done. Don't put off until tomorrow what you can do today. Looks like the FI metric lineup has nothing but power hitters. Another home run for FI metric.

And the traditionalists? They claim to be respectful of the importance of time, but then they put you on a 40 year plan for retirement. It's hypocrisy. Say one thing out of this side of your mouth and then say something else out the other. The fixed rate savings idea and the consumption smoothing idea don't respect time. They stretch it out as long as possible. The traditional approach to financial planning might claim to honor the importance of time, but in practice they fail to follow through.

FI metric wins again. Score: 4-0.

5. Realize that you are in charge: FI metric is a framework. It encourages you to take charge of your own finances. To not entrust your future to somebody else. I've used the analogy of the FI metric system being the car and you being the driver. Yes, with FI metric you are most definitely in charge. Nobody knows or cares about your finances as much as you do. You must remain in charge of your finances and the FI metric system encourages you to do so.

The traditionalists want you to trust them. They think they have the best plan. Just increase your FICO score and everything will be all right. Just pay off your credit debt and you will be good to go. Just save 15% of your income and you are on the right track. In other words, they tell you to trust them rather than to take charge. They want you to buy their latest book. A couple years later, they will have another book which explains why now they really have the answer.

Once again FI metric destroys the competition. Final score: 6-0.

So there you go. I put the FI metric system up against the competition using an unbiased standard of financial planning best practices. I honestly think that the FI metric system wins in every single category. Yes, it's new. Yes, it's different. But the system works. It is effective and efficient. It meets all of the best practices.

So, you stand at a fork in the road. You have a decision to make. Should you commit to the FI metric framework or not? I don't know what more I can do to convince you. The ball is in your court. If you decide that the FI metric system is not for you, then I still wish you the best of luck. I hope you can accomplish your goals using whatever system you decide to go with. For those of you gladiators who are ready for a life change, commit to the FI metric system. Get going right away. The clock is ticking on all of us. Will you join me and cross the finish line to financial independence? The choice is yours. Here's wishing you a very high FI!

AFTERWORD

If you really want to jump into the FI metric system, then there is no better way to do it than to use the FImetric online software package to manage your personal finances. It implements everything in the FI metric system. It will make easy work of creating your balance sheet and computing your FI every month. The FI metric software package is an available at *http://www.fimetric.com*. Sign up for your free account today and join the financial independence revolution. Do your friends and family a great favor too and get them started on the path to sound financial management. Somewhere down the road, they will thank you for getting them on the right track.

ABOUT THE AUTHOR

Eric Holland is a software developer, financial advisor and entrepreneur. He has degrees in Computer Science and Finance. He is a Certified Public Account and an Enrolled Agent. You can read his blog at *www.PersonalFinanceAnswerMan.com* where he writes about financial freedom and the FI metric.

Eric is also the owner of FImetric Corporation. FImetric has an excellent online software package for managing personal finances. It does much more than Quicken or Mint or any other financial management system because it implements the FI metric system. Rather than just balancing your checkbook and categorizing your expenses, FImetric focuses on increasing your FI. Check it out at *http://www.fimetric.com.*

www.ingramcontent.com/pod-product-compliance
Lightning Source LLC
Chambersburg PA
CBHW051526170526
45165CB00002B/627